Dora Mills

The boy who came back
from heaven

KEVIN & ALEX MALARKEY

The boy who came back from heaven

A remarkable account of miracles, angels,
and life beyond this world

TYNDALE HOUSE PUBLISHERS, INC.
CAROL STREAM, ILLINOIS

The Library of Congress has catalogued the hardcover edition as follows:

Malarkey, Kevin.
  The boy who came back from heaven : a remarkable account of miracles, angels, and life beyond this world / Kevin and Alex Malarkey.
    p. cm.
  ISBN 978-1-4143-3606-0 (hc)
    1. Near-death experiences—Religious aspects—Christianity.   2. Malarkey, Alex.   3. Heaven—Christianity.   4. Future life—Christianity.   I. Malarkey, Alex.   II. Title.
  BT833.M35 2010
  236'.1092—dc22
  [B]   2010018732

ISBN 978-1-4143-3607-7 (sc)
Printed in the United States of America

17   16   15   14   13   12   11
14   13   12   11

Contents

Acknowledgments

How could Alex and I thank anyone before thanking God in Heaven, who saved both of our lives on November 14, 2004, and who is the reason we have the meaning and hope that permeates our lives?

Thanks to Beth, who had a vision for what Alex's story could do to help others. Her tireless work on Alex's behalf goes beyond any description. Thank you, Aaron, Gracie, and Ryan, for always striving to understand the attention that Alex gets while also understanding that God, your mom, and I care for you every bit as much as your big brother.

Thank you to the thousands and thousands of people who have prayed on a daily basis for many years for our family. You have played an important role, which we have attempted to show in our story. More important than this, your prayers are stored in Heaven. Thank you, Pastor Brown, Pastor Ricks, and all of the other amazing people who organized efforts to help our family.

Thank you to all of the incredible people at Tyndale House who not only turned our story into a book, but who themselves have become key members of the prayer support for Alex and the rest of our crew. Alex would like to make special mention of his buddy Stephen Vosloo, who worked on all the pictures for the book and who has continually brought a smile to

Alex's face since the day they met. Thank you to Lisa Jackson, Kim Miller, and Jan Long Harris for helping us organize our story. Thanks, too, to Rob Suggs for your help on the manuscript.

Thank you, Matt Jacobson, for—what haven't you done?—praying, writing, editing, and serving us as our agent and, most importantly, as our friend.

I would also like to thank my parents for always believing in me and for introducing me to the God I now serve. Thanks also to Beth's parents, who have taught me about courage and grace during hard times.

Lastly, I would like to thank my son Alex. You are my hero and the person I most want to be like when I grow up.

Introduction

WE WERE MADE for so much more than the things of this world.

Sometimes we can sense this. We have a feeling that, despite our best efforts, we don't quite belong here, that this is not our final destination. We have deep hungers and thirsts that cannot yet be satisfied.

In fact, when we try to make this world our home, our ultimate security and place of comfort, we simply end up feeling disappointed or empty. This is why a great saint of the church was moved to write, "Our hearts are restless until they find their rest in Thee."

Our home is Heaven. But what is Heaven? Heaven radiates with the brilliance of God's glory. It is filled with the music of angels in worship and the beauty of an unmarred landscape. Because it is the dwelling place of God, those who enter its gates experience only peace, hope, faith, and love—the very essence of God Himself.

Much as we long for Heaven, there is a problem. We know very little of the place where we were made to live. Whom do you know who has been there? Have you seen any photographs? Sure, you may have heard stories of white light and tunnels from people who have experienced death and then returned to this life. But what if there was a person who had been to Heaven . . . *actually walked through the gates* . . . and stayed long enough to learn about it? Would you be interested in what he had to say?

Well, I know such a person. He is my son, William Alexander Malarkey. We call him Alex.

In November 2004, Alex and I were in a car accident. The accident was so horrific that Alex, who was six at the time, was not expected to live, and a medical officer suggested that the coroner be called to the scene. Later, in the hospital, Alex was in a coma for two months. Alex spent time during this period in Heaven, and when he returned to us, he had much to say about his experience.

Now, I know what you may be thinking: *A kid goes to Heaven and comes back to tell us about it? Come on.*

I'm not here to beat a drum, convince you of a theological argument, or force you to validate Alex's experiences. But I humbly offer a challenge: suspend your judgment for just a few chapters.

I think your life may be changed forever.

Sometimes I have no clue what to make of Alex's supernatural life—I have no theological box to put some of this stuff in. But everyone who has taken the time to get to know Alex agrees: he is a remarkable boy on whom God has placed His hand for His purposes.

What follows includes physical descriptions of parts of Heaven, a recounting of the way Alex and God sometimes talk face-to-face, and details about Alex's direct experience with angels, demons, and, yes, the devil himself.

Heaven is real. There is an unseen world at work—an intensely active spiritual dimension right here on earth, all around us. And much of this activity keeps us from focusing on our future destination, the place where we will spend eternity.

Alex has been there. And if your heart is ever restless, if you've ever longed for more than this world offers, I invite you to follow Alex on his journey to Heaven and back.

CHAPTER I

AT THE CROSSROADS

The straight, empty road was a deadly optical illusion.

THE LEAVES BARELY clung to the old oaks lining the highway that cool November morning. As Alex and I drove to church in my old Honda Civic, I finally began to relax from the sense of hurry I had felt while getting my oldest son dressed and out the door.

In our family, as in many others, getting organized to go to church involved fighting the forces of chaos. We had already been running late when Alex streaked through the house in his birthday suit to sit and watch a nature show on TV instead of getting dressed, as he had been told to do. No clothes, no breakfast, and, truthfully, no obedience to Mommy all added up to strained nerves and short tempers. But much more than this was going on in our family.

Only the day before, our newborn, Ryan, had come home from the hospital. That put the count at four children, ages six and under. Can anyone truly be ready for four young children? It seemed that the best way to preserve some sense of normalcy was for at least two of us to make it to church that day.

Now, glancing into the rearview mirror, I smiled as Alex's eyes danced back at me.

"Hey, buddy, I'm glad you're with me today."

"Me too, Daddy. This is Daddy-Alex time, isn't it?"

"That's right, Alex. Just you and me!"

Alex was my buddy. From the beginning, we had done everything and gone everywhere together. Never too far away were several of Alex's "Barneys." Some kids have a fuzzy animal. Some kids have a security blanket. Alex had his "Barneys"—small cloths he liked to chew on. Six-year-old Alex was my oldest of four—*four!* What a huge number! Now that was going to take some getting used to.

We drove on in silence. As if involuntarily peering into the future, my eyes fixed on the horizon, on a future that seemed filled with equal measures of richness and, frankly, uncertainty. The full weight of the responsibility of being "Daddy" to four young children pressed against me. The deep breath I unwittingly sucked in burst out in a loud exhale. I couldn't help but think about the medical bills.

We had recently switched medical insurance providers and wouldn't be covered for pregnancy for a few more months. To arrive without insurance coverage didn't make our new little boy any less wonderful, but there was no getting around it—it did make his coming brutally expensive.

Leaves blew across the highway, the evidence of a stiffening breeze. The season was changing. *Everything* was changing—new home, new church, new baby. Seasons—they are natural and good. We were embarking on a new season in our family—another child. It was natural and good too. Things would work out with the money. They always did. The quick refocus brought a sense of reassurance and helped me savor what had happened just yesterday: my beautiful wife, Beth, and I had filled the hours with multiple turns of holding, touching, and cooing over our newborn.

Alex hadn't wanted to.

"Come here, Alex," I said. "You're his big brother. Come hold baby Ryan."

"Daddy, I don't really want to. Can I just hold the camera? I'm not into holding babies."

I studied my oldest child for a moment and traded glances with Beth.

"Sure, Son; here, you hold the camera."

Who can figure out the mind of a little boy? He'd grow close to baby Ryan in his own time. Why force him?

Pulling into the church parking lot brought me back to the present. Beth and the new baby were now resting at home with Gracie, age two, and Aaron, four, and Alex and I were about to meet some new people. We had only attended this church a few times.

Before I left the car, it struck me in a fresh way how much I really did have to be thankful for, how much I had been blessed, how much I'd been given: we had a new member of our family at the same time we were becoming members of a new church family, having moved to a new home in the country not long before. Even though my psychotherapy private practice had been slow lately, I did have an occupation—unlike many people we knew who were struggling greatly.

But was I truly thankful? Yes, kind of . . . in a general sense. The continual pressure of ever-mounting bills has a way of demanding attention, of obscuring all the good things from view, of distorting the beauty that surrounds us and fills our lives. It's like an annoying drip from the faucet that you just can't fix, or in my case, like the piercing screech of a smoke detector, warning of the smaller bills that hadn't been paid and of the mortgage payment that still hadn't been sent . . . for the second month. The truth is, the cloud of that financial pressure obscured the beautiful, crisp sunshine of God's truths for me. Even so, it was Sunday, and on Sunday in our family, you go to church.

With Alex off to his class, I took a seat. I smiled politely at everyone who made eye contact as they looked for seats in the auditorium, but my mind was consumed, again, with an image of our bill basket, which seemed to glare at me every time I walked through the front door at home. The singing stopped, and suddenly I was back in the present with Pastor Gary Brown opening his Bible on the pulpit as he began to speak:

"We have been exploring different aspects of the character of God. God has identified Himself in Scripture by using many names. Today we are considering how God has revealed Himself to us relative to our needs: Jehovah-jireh. Ensuring we have what we need is a responsibility that God takes on Himself, a message He gives by His name, which means, literally, 'the Lord will provide.' Let's be clear: God didn't say He would provide for all our wants but for things He believes we need. If God has said that our needs are His concern and responsibility, why do we spend so much time being anxious?"

I felt as if there were a bull's-eye painted on my forehead with a large dart sticking into it. The sermon could have ended right there. My burden, so palpable moments before, was replaced by a lightness of spirit I hadn't known all morning. This was only my fifth visit to the church, so there was no way Pastor Brown could have consciously tailored his sermon to my situation. My head fell into my hands, and I had to smile at the timeliness of the rebuke. God is the Provider. He knows what I need. I thought again about our bill basket. *First thing I'm doing when I get home is tape a big sign on the front of it: God Will Meet Our Needs.*

Following the service, I got into a conversation with the children's pastor. We walked the lawn in the now-pleasant late-autumn air, discussing the vision of the pastor and staff for this church. Alex tried to be patient during this adult conversation. We exchanged glances and smiled at each other, but it was tough for my little guy to endure a conversation that, for him, felt as if it would never end. I leaned down and whispered, "Alex, you're such a good boy. Let's find a park on the way home, okay?"

A big grin signaled his approval.

A few minutes later, Alex and I made our way back to the car, now virtually alone in the parking lot. I buckled him into the backseat, but before getting behind the wheel, I let my eyes wander across the pavement to the front doors of the church building. I had come with anxiety and was leaving with hope. How could I not give thanks?

"Remember, Daddy, we have to go to a park!" Alex called as I got in the driver's seat.

"You bet, Alex. But you have to help me find one. Keep a sharp eye out your window."

We drove down the road looking for the elusive playground with the intensity of hunters stalking big game.

During the short drive, a cemetery came into view. I had often used the appearance of a cemetery to teach Alex that we each have a spirit. "Hey, look, Alex, a graveyard. What's in there?"

"Just bodies, Daddy. Graveyards don't have people, 'cause when they die, their spirits leave their bodies and go to their new home."

"You got it, Son. Now, where's that park?"

Before long, Alex shouted, "Look, there's one. Over there!"

The car had barely stopped before Alex jumped out on a dead run to the ladders, bars, and chutes. It was only a few months back at some burger joint that Alex had lost his nerve on the top of the tube slide. There I was, squeezing my six-foot-two frame through the tunnel—Dad to the rescue! Not anymore. Somehow since then, Alex had transformed into the Daredevil Kid. "Alex, be careful," I warned. "You're scaring me. Watch where you're putting your hands and feet."

Beth was usually on hand to keep a lid on things, but with her absent, I suddenly felt Alex was taking way too many risks. I had good reason. Alex was already a two-time veteran visitor to the emergency room. On his last visit, I do have to admit that Alex's timing was good. There I was in emergency, getting Alex stitched up. When the doctor was finished, I passed Alex off to his aunt and hoofed it to the birthing room to be with Beth just before Aaron arrived! The way Alex was swinging, hanging, and balancing now, it was easy to imagine another visit today.

"Daddy, look, no hands!"

"You're a champ, Alex. Now be careful." Where was my timid little Alex?

After about fifteen minutes, I started to get antsy, knowing Beth would be wondering where we were.

"Come on, buddy. We'd better get home. Mommy is already wondering what happened to us."

Between Heaven and Earth

After securing Alex in the seat directly behind mine, I pulled the strap to make sure it was tight. The next challenge was to find our way home through this unfamiliar territory—not that I didn't know how I got to the church, but finding shortcuts and exploring new roads are all part of the fun of living in a new area. I pulled out onto the road, and a short distance ahead, an intersection came into view. I began dialing my cell phone to let Beth know where we were.

"Hey, Alex, I'll bet that road will get us home. Let's take it." Though a rural road, it was bordered by several ranch-style houses with deep front yards.

Ring . . . Ring . . .

Stopped at the intersection with the phone to my ear, I looked both directions—as always. No oncoming traffic for at least half a mile. What I didn't know was that at this unfamiliar intersection I was not looking down a perfectly straight half-mile stretch of road. Several hundred yards ahead, just before the road curved off to the left, was a huge dip that obscured anything that might have been there. The straight, empty road was a deadly optical illusion.

"Hey, Beth, how's it going? . . . Well, I got into a long conversation after the service, and then we found a park, but we're on our way home now. We should be there . . ."

"Dad, I'm hungry. When are we going to be home?"

I turned to answer Alex while still on the phone with Beth. I pulled into the intersection and then . . .

The deafening crunch of metal ripping metal flashed and then faded into brilliant silence. All was silence.

+++

As unconsciousness yielded to confused awareness, my mind strove to bring order from chaos. The meager beginning of a thought forced its way into clarity: *Why am I lying in a ditch next to my car?* My mind raced. *What is going on?* With the first light of reason flickering in my still foggy mind, I sat up, bewildered. What had happened? Why was I here? Alex—he was with me, wasn't he? *Where is Alex? Where is my boy?*

I do not know how long I was unconscious, but several people had already run from the nearby homes to the accident site. "Lie still. Don't move," someone implored. I couldn't. Every fiber of my heart was screaming, *Where is Alex?* Now that I was on my feet, everything sounded muffled. I was moving in slow motion, as if I were walking on the bottom of a swimming pool. Over and over I yelled, *"Alex, Alex, Alex!"* No answer. My heart pounded out a rhythm of fear. The silence fell like a hammer but was soon pierced by the wail of sirens.

Just as my mind was being overthrown by fear, a gentle arm wrapped around my shoulder. I turned to look into the kind eyes of a total stranger.

"You've been in a car accident, son. There is a young boy still in the backseat of the car."

Firemen and policemen swarmed everywhere, concentrating on what used to be my car. Before I had a moment's thought about what I might find in the backseat, I ran over and looked. An acrid, evil smell violated my senses. Amidst thousands of glass shards, torn upholstery, and twisted metal, there sat my boy, my firstborn son, on whom his mother and father's dreams rested, still strapped in his seatbelt—still in his church clothes. *He's okay, he's okay. He's been knocked unconscious and probably has a concussion, but he's going to be okay.* But in that moment of desperation, what I frantically hoped was no match for harsh reality. And as I continued to stare, dread soon overcame my hope. Blood ran from a gash on Alex's forehead. And what was wrong with his head? It hung so unnaturally down to the left, bizarrely lower than it should have been. Vacant, hideously bloodshot eyes stared down.

Alex, my son . . . he looks dead! I've killed my son.

An immense wave of incredulity, horror, and crushing grief loomed above me, threatening to swallow me. On the other side of the car, the paramedics worked furiously, trying to remove Alex and get him onto a stretcher, all the while attempting to establish an airway in order to get oxygen into his lungs.

Moments later, a senior medical officer consulting with the policeman who was first on the scene said, "We'll need to contact the coroner's office and cancel MedFlight."

"Yes, sir, but the chopper's already landing."

Panic stabbed my chest and breath came in short gasps as my mind raced uncontrollably through the mayhem: *I'm the cause of all this. Have I killed my son? What about the people in the other car? Where did that car come from? Am I going to jail? Is Alex really dead?*

+++ I heard a mighty crash at the intersection only a few dozen yards from my front door. I had been a fireman and thought I might be able to help, so I sprinted toward the accident scene. When I arrived, Kevin, whom I didn't know at the time, was in a daze. People were urging him to sit down, as he was obviously disoriented. I first went up to the other car, but those people all seemed to be okay. I then went over to

Kevin's car and could see that a little boy was in the backseat. I climbed in the back as best I could, but I had no idea if the little boy was dead or alive. I knew enough not to touch his head but placed my hand over his chest. There was no perceptible breathing. I'm a man of faith, so I started praying for this little guy. I also talked to him as if he could hear me, although there was no response. I said, "Hey, little guy, don't worry."

And I kept praying.

"You're going to be all right."

And I kept praying.

"Don't be afraid. You just hang in there."

And I kept praying.

"You're going to make it, buddy. Help is on the way."

I didn't have any indication that Alex was alive, but I kept praying for him and his dad.

Dan Tullis +++

As bystanders gathered around the organized confusion of the rescue effort, shame poured over me—the father who had caused destruction in so many lives. Were all these people secretly condemning me? They were too late. Condemnation had already invaded the very recesses of my heart. *Oh God, what have I done?*

Fear coursed through my body like an electrical surge. Utterly bewildered as to what to do, I turned when a hand on my right shoulder interrupted my thoughts.

"Sir, we found this cell phone in the car. Would you like to call your wife?"

Beth! Oh, no! She was on the phone with me when the accident occurred. She was still at home with two-day-old baby Ryan and Aaron and Gracie. What was she thinking? What did she hear? While dialing the number, I willed down the rising tightness in my throat.

"Beth."

"Hello, Kevin?"

But the moment her voice fell on my ear, grief and shame burst out in gasping sobs.

"Oh, Beth, oh, Beth, we've been in a terrible accident!" Tears streamed down my face.

"Is he dead?" she asked, her voice low and calm.

"I don't know. I don't know. They're loading him in a chopper and taking him to Children's. I'm so sorry, Beth."

"I've got the kids. Let's just stay focused on what we need to do right now. I'll meet you at Children's."

In the precise mayhem of the rescue effort, I heard someone say, "We've got a heartbeat—super weak, but it's there." By then Beth had hung up the phone and was gathering the children to make the hour-and-a-half-long trek to Columbus Children's Hospital.

I ran to the chopper, determined that I was coming on that trip, too, but a strong arm reached out, stopping me.

"Are you the father?" asked a uniformed medic.

"Yes, yes, I am," I said, trying to surge ahead and board the chopper.

"You're welcome to ride with us." But then he hesitated for a moment and looked back over the accident scene.

+++

On the drive down, I remember telling God, "Alex is Yours. If You decide to take him home, that's okay, but You have to give me the strength to do this."

Beth Malarkey, Alex's mom

11

"Pardon me, but were you in the accident too?"
"Yes, I was driving but came out fine."

+++ Time is always of the essence, but more so in Alex's case. When we first assessed Alex at the accident scene, his pupils were fixed (not responding to light), he was not breathing on his own, and it was difficult to feel his pulse. My partner and I knew he was severely injured and thought he would probably die from his injuries. Even so we did our best. On the way to the accident, I had felt in my heart that I needed to pray before we arrived, so I had prayed quietly as we flew to the scene. Now I better understood why.

Once we had Alex on a cot, we carried him back to the helicopter. Kevin asked if he could pray with his son before we left. We told him he could, but he needed to be quick because we really needed to go. Kevin broke down, and we became concerned that his prayer would take too long. I asked him if he was a Christian, and he said he was. I told him the nurse and I were too. I asked him if he believed God wanted to heal his son, and he said he did. I told him that we believed that too. After that, I asked him if he would allow me to pray for his son in the helicopter. He said yes, so we thanked him and left.

Once we got into the helicopter, I quickly laid my hand on Alex's head and prayed that he would be healed in the name of Jesus. Then I simply thanked the Lord for healing Alex and believed that God was doing what He said He would do in His Word.

I often pray for patients in-flight—not every time, but often.

Dave Knopp, paramedic +++

"I'm so sorry, sir, but you can't come with us then. You need to be examined at our local hospital."

Panic gripped me again. Not go with Alex? Impossible! I was reduced to begging but didn't care. "You've got to let me go with my son. Really, I'm okay. I've got to. Please let me go with Alex . . . please?"

"Sir, I understand how you may be feeling, but right now the best thing you can do for your son is go to the hospital, get checked out, and make sure you're okay, and let us do what we need to do. Alex is your priority. He's ours, too."

"But I'm okay!" I protested. "Look, I'm walking around fine. You've got to let me go with him."

Firmly but respectfully, the paramedic said, "I'm sorry, sir. I have to shut the doors and go now."

"Oh God, oh God!" I cried out, frantically praying, "Please save my little boy, please . . ." But that's all I got out as sobs of grief enveloped me.

The first medic looked at his partner and said with tightened jaw, "We have to go now."

From Alex

I Went to Heaven

Let the children come to me. Don't stop them! For the Kingdom of God belongs to those who are like these children.

MARK 10:14

Daddy did not see the car coming, but I did. I like to look out the back side window of Daddy's car, and so that is what I was doing when we started to turn. I was just getting ready to tell him there was a car when we got hit.

For just one second before all of the "action" began, there was a moment of calmness. I remember thinking someone was going to die. When the calm ended, I heard the sound of glass breaking, and I saw Daddy's feet going out of the car.

Now I thought I knew who was going to die. But then I saw something unbelievably cool. Five angels were carrying Daddy outside the car. Four were carrying his body, and one was supporting his neck and head. The angels were big and muscular, like wrestlers, and they had wings on their backs from their waists to their shoulders. I thought Daddy was dead, but that it was okay because the angels were going to make him okay.

Then I looked to the front passenger seat, and the devil was looking into my eyes. He said, "Yeah, that's right, your daddy is dead, and it is your fault." I thought the accident was my fault because I had asked Daddy a question and he turned to answer my question right before the car hit us. I'm not sure whether I watched Daddy from the car or from Heaven. I went to Heaven shortly after the car hit us, but I am not sure of the exact moment I actually left my body. I do know that when I was in Heaven, everything was perfect.

This is what happened in the car after the other car hit us. All of this happened in what seemed to be a few seconds. I heard the sound of shattering glass, and I tried to duck my head to protect myself. As I ducked down, I saw a piece of glass in my thumb. That is when I realized that all of this was real. I tried to bite down on Barney. I felt a pain in my mouth like, maybe, I had bitten through my tongue. I began to feel pain throughout my body. I thought that I would be the next one to die. I thought that there was some fire behind me because my back felt like it was burning. I tried to turn my head toward the back of the car, but there was no fire. I could only see a big black circle, and something smelled really nasty. I felt a bad pain in the back of my head. It felt like a knife stabbing my neck. Then I realized that my head was hanging down to one side and I could not lift it back up.

I tried to call out to my daddy, but I couldn't hear the sound of my voice. I thought that maybe my hearing wasn't working. Then I thought the sound of the car hitting us was echoing in my head. With my lips I said, "I love you, Daddy."

I thought the roof of the car was going to collapse on me. I felt like I was in a plane that was flying on the road. It sounded like a volcano was erupting and coming my way. I saw the two air bags blow up. Daddy flew out of the car right before the air bags came out. The window on the passenger side in the front of the car broke. The backseat was torn up by flying glass. There was glass in my right hand, in my left armpit, in my hair, and in my private place. I knew my eyebrow was cut because blood was dripping down. I knew I was bleeding in my throat, my nose, and my eyes. I felt like I was bleeding in my stomach, too, from the seatbelt.

The fireman cut my seatbelt off because it was jammed. They put something in my throat to make me breathe. While I was on the stretcher, they told me to be strong. They said that I was hurt badly and that I was going to the hospital. They said I was a tough boy.

I went through a long, white tunnel that was very bright. I didn't like the music in the tunnel; it was really bad music played on instruments with really long strings.

But then I got to Heaven, and there was powerful music, and I loved it.

When I arrived in Heaven, the same five angels who had helped Daddy out of the car were there. They comforted me. Daddy was in Heaven too. The angels stayed with me so Daddy could be alone with God. Daddy had bad injuries like mine, but God was healing him in Heaven to bring glory to Himself—that's what God told me later. Daddy asked God if he could trade places with me, but God said no. God said He would heal me later on earth to bring more glory to His name.

After God said no to Daddy, Daddy's spirit returned to his body next to our smashed car. I could see Daddy from Heaven, lying in the ditch next to our car.[1]

---

[1] Kevin: "I have no memory of being in Heaven, but Alex is emphatic that this is what happened."

CHAPTER 2

THREE JOURNEYS

I had been impatient to get to Alex,
but could I handle what awaited me?

TEARS STREAMED DOWN my face as the doors of the chopper slammed shut. As it began its ascent, I stood back, wondering, *Will I ever see my little boy alive again?* Yes, that's it. I had to get to Children's Hospital immediately.

"Excuse me, sir. Could you please come with me?"

I glanced around at the voice, half dazed and still watching the helicopter recede farther into the blue.

"Sir, excuse me," continued the paramedic. "Can you come with me?"

While he was still speaking, a stretcher appeared from somewhere and the second paramedic said, "Please, lie down here."

"Why do I need to lie down?" I protested. My thoughts were now wholly turned to getting to Children's Hospital as soon as possible.

"We need to get you to the hospital, sir."

"Me? Hospital? Why do I need to go to the hospital? My son needs to go, and he just left. I'm sorry, but I've got to get to Children's in Columbus immediately. Alex needs me."

For all their politeness, a quick exchange of glances between the paramedics betrayed their determination to take me to the hospital.

"Sir, you've been in a major accident," one of them said. "You need to be seen by a doctor, and going into shock after an event such as this is not uncommon. Thank you for coming with us." He smiled.

I felt frantic, like a caged animal. My heart started to race again. *I can't go somewhere else. I have to get to Alex!* That surge of desperation almost caused me to stand my ground, but I could see that they were resolute. I reasoned that the fastest way to get to Alex was to cooperate and get this over with as quickly as possible. And yes, I probably was in a mild state of shock—but it seemed to me that it was everyone else who was being irrational. Walking toward the ambulance, I realized for the first time that I had a severe limp in my right leg. A sharp pain stabbed my neck when I turned one last time to look at the accident scene.

Finally I let the attendants load me onto the stretcher and into the ambulance. We were off to some local hospital, sirens blaring, and traveling at about four miles per hour, or so it seemed to me. As I lay on my back, staring at the ceiling of the ambulance, my emotions lurched sporadically in every direction: anger, shame, hope, denial, grief. In the end, fear and shame took center stage. Would the next time I saw Alex be in some morbid funeral parlor? How could Beth keep from hating me for what I had done to Alex? What had I done to our family? Shouldn't I hate myself? This was totally my fault. How could I have been so careless?

In the midst of this mental bombardment, my mind faded to gray and went blank. Shock enveloped me like an impenetrable fog, cushioning my tormented mind from a reality too harsh to face.

+++

Before long, I was sitting on the edge of a bed in the emergency room of a local hospital. A nurse impassively drew blood from my left forearm—a procedure legally, not medically, driven. The blood sample would establish my level of sobriety. Had this father killed his son because he couldn't stay off the bottle? At least I was innocent on that count.

Bearing away my blood samples, the nurse closed the door behind her, and for the first time since regaining consciousness, I was completely alone. Everything was quiet except for the muffled sound of voices in the adjacent room. Rubbing my neck caused a sharp pain, and suddenly the memory of the other car leaped into my mind. What about the people in the other car? I'd never seen the car, never anticipated it, and now I began worrying about the people who were in it—on top of everything else.

The door suddenly swung open.

"What happened to the other car? The people in the other car— how are they?" I blurted out.

"Doing okay. Matter of fact, they're in the next room," said the staffer, pointing a thumb toward the wall. Though I couldn't make out the words, hearing those voices plunged me into a new round of despair. My carelessness had visited misfortune upon people I didn't even know. The shame pressed against my ribs like a giant vise, forcing me to breathe in short, inadequate gasps. Two competing impulses overtook my thoughts: Couldn't I become invisible and just float out the window, away from this entire day? And yet I needed to rush into the next room, fall on my knees, and beg for forgiveness, for mercy, telling the other driver and passengers how deeply sorry I was and showing them I wasn't some irresponsible monster.

In the end, I just stared at the wall where the voices seemed to be coming from. If I had gone in there, it would have been about salving my conscience. I was the last person they wanted to see right now. What did it matter to them who had caused the accident and how that driver felt about it?

In the meantime, another nurse had entered my room and was attempting to get my attention. "Will you follow me, sir? We need to take a few X-rays."

I followed again and sat restlessly in another waiting room. Hearing a noise, I turned to the door and looked into the eyes of Pastor Brown, who had learned of the accident from a church member who was a nurse at the hospital. His very presence brought peace to my heart in a moment of turmoil I could not control. He sat down beside me, wrapping a consoling arm around my shoulder.

"Kevin, I know you're anxious about your family. They're all on their way to Children's Hospital right now. They've been told that you came out of it okay."

"Pastor, I've got to get out of here now and get over to Children's. I've got to see Alex. They're keeping me here too long. How long before I can get out of here?"

The pastor, understanding how I felt, nodded. "A friend of yours is in the main waiting room right now," he said. "He's on standby to take you to Columbus as soon as this place releases you."

"Thanks, Pastor. You guys are great to look out for me."

+++

The X-rays showed no serious damage, so I was directed back to the emergency room . . . to wait. Thoughts of Alex renewed my sense of urgency to leave. The door swung open again. I looked up.

"Mr. Malarkey . . ." said the doctor, flanked by two nurses.

"Yes, Doctor."

"We need to keep you overnight for observation. My staff here will make sure you are comfortable."

The nurses smiled and nodded their heads. Their smiles faded as I rose to my feet and looked directly into each person's eyes, starting with the doctor. If there was one thing I wasn't going to do, it was to stay away from Alex for one moment longer. This I made clear—politely, I hope. They seemed to understand that I was resolute and, after a few halfhearted protests about what was best, relented.

I quickly gathered my things and all but ran to the lobby—slowed only by the limp from the accident. Rounding the corner, I saw Kelly before he saw me. I didn't know Kelly well since we had not been living in this community long, but even so, I could tell he was crestfallen, like he wished he didn't know what he knew. He brightened, though, upon seeing me.

"Oh, hey, Kevin. I can drive you to the hospital."

"Great," I said, "thanks."

Kelly looked at me somewhat quizzically. "Do you want to stop by your house to get some clothes?"

I was so focused on getting to Alex's side that I had forgotten (or was I still in shock?) that I was in the hospital gown—the kind with built-in air-conditioning in the back. My clothes had been cut from my body and were in the sack under my arm.

"Here," Kelly offered, holding out his leather jacket. Hospital gown and leather jacket—I was now dressed for the trip home.

Arriving at the house sent eerie chills through my chest. I knew no one would be there. Even so, the house seemed especially dark, silent, empty. As I looked at the toys scattered across the room, I suddenly realized I hadn't talked to my children and only very briefly to Beth. What was she feeling? What had the children been told? What did they know?

I'm the man of the family. I was supposed to protect my wife and kids. I wasn't with them, wasn't protecting them, and wasn't comforting them. I was the cause of everything. The darkness of my spirit descended like an angry cloud over my heart. The voice of fear whispered, *Beth will hate you for doing this to your family.* Shame for the present and fear for the future pierced my heart like talons from the darkness. The mocking voice threatened to drown out all others. Kelly's presence was God's provision for me.

Like a continuously looping video, scenes of the accident—or at least as much as I could remember—played in my mind again and again as Kelly drove me to Columbus. There were so many gaps that I ended up in confusion with each new attempt to understand. For some time, Kelly was respectfully quiet, but finally he broke the silence.

"You know, Kevin, from my house, the accident site is on the way to the hospital."

"So you drove by there on the way to pick me up?"

"Yes, I did," Kelly said gravely.

"What do you think?"

After a short pause, Kelly continued, his eyes growing moist. "It was really bad, Kevin."

"What do you think about Alex?" I asked, desperately looking for some reassurance.

"It's hard to say. Let's see what we find out at the hospital."

Kelly wanted to prepare me for what might be, but he tried not to be specific. That would never do for me. I needed answers.

"I need to know what you think, Kelly. Do you think Alex is all right?" Somehow it was important for me to hear him say what his face already revealed.

"Kevin, I don't think Alex made it. I think that Alex has gone to be with Jesus. I am so sorry, brother."

I looked out the window as my eyes instantly brimmed with tears, choking back the pain of those words. My heart was breaking. *God, I can't take this. Please don't make me say good-bye—not this way. Not because I drove out in front of an oncoming car. Oh, God, please save my boy. Please save my firstborn son, my little buddy, Alex.*

For the next few miles, while Kelly drove on in silence, waves of pain and grief battered my heart. In the midst of it all, a lone, small voice from somewhere deep within made the case that Kelly couldn't be certain of Alex's condition—*Don't stop praying for Alex. Don't stop.*

We pulled up to Children's Hospital. Kelly parked, turned off the engine, paused, and looked at me.

"Are you going to be okay?"

"This is hard, Kelly." I grimaced, taking in a deep breath. "You know, Beth and I have driven by here a hundred times. We've often talked about how sad a place it is—how we hoped we'd never have to go in there. And now here we are."

In minutes, I would meet Beth inside those walls. All the countless times Beth had told me to slow down and pay more attention to the road flooded my mind. She had warned me dozens of times to be more cautious, to be more careful with the kids, especially in play activities with Alex and Aaron. I'd always thought she was so overprotective and spent far too much time worrying. It wasn't that long ago that I had said, "Hey, relax. I didn't kill them." How those words haunted me now as I braced myself to face her.

Strength under Pressure

My Beth is one amazing woman. Only one day home from giving birth to our fourth child, she needed to rest and recuperate, but instead she hung up from my phone call and went into high gear, getting the children ready for the hour-and-a-half drive to the hospital in Columbus, which was sixty-five miles away. Many people fall apart under pressure. Not Beth. In the midst of the most stressful situations, Beth is all composure. There may be a raging fire of emotion in her heart, but more than anyone I know, she has the capacity to completely subdue those natural emotions and do what needs to be done without giving the slightest indication of the trauma that has overtaken her. What an amazing blessing these qualities were now.

Beth hadn't thought too much of the line going dead on our original phone call; we live in a rural area and this happens fairly frequently. The second call was obviously a different matter. God had prepared Beth to some degree for this moment by helping her to endure a variety of previous struggles. Simply put, my wife is able to thrive in difficult situations.

Beth did not need to say anything to our two-day-old son or our two-year-old daughter about the circumstances; they wouldn't understand what she was talking about. She did tell our four-year-old, Aaron, that there had been a car accident and that they needed to get to the hospital to see his brother. Aaron cried, and she was able to comfort him for the moment. She then packed the three kids into the van and set out for the hospital.

While en route, Beth received a phone call from the emergency room at Children's.

"Is this Mrs. Malarkey, mother of Alex Malarkey?"

"Yes, it is."

"Mrs. Malarkey, could you tell us if Alex is allergic to any medicines?"

For the second time, Beth asked an essential question, "Is my son going to live?" And for the second time the answer she received was maddeningly vague.

"It is serious, Mrs. Malarkey."

+++

When Mommy told me Alex was hurt bad, I was scared out of my brains and didn't know what to do. I thought Mommy was lying when she said Alex might be dead because I didn't think that could be true.

Aaron Malarkey, Alex's brother

Soon after, Beth called her sister, Kris. She told her the little she knew of the situation. Kris is a registered nurse and a wonderfully supportive and empathetic person. After a brief conversation, Beth returned to her driving. She says she never drove over the speed limit during the entire drive, and I believe her. In fact, I have never seen her speed. That's Beth: a rock under pressure.

As Beth pulled into the parking lot at the hospital, she spotted a man wearing a MedFlight uniform. She quickly backed up, rolled down the window, and called out to him, "I have a six-year-old son who just arrived by helicopter. Were you on that flight?"

The man walked over to her. "Yes, ma'am. My name's Dave."

"Is my son all right? How bad was it?"

Looking into Beth's eyes, Dave said, "I have a question for you."

"Yes?" Beth said quizzically.

"Are you a Christian?"

"Yes, I am," Beth answered, wondering where this was going.

"Then listen to me," Dave continued, intently looking into Beth's eyes. "You're going to go in the trauma room and you're going to hear some horrible things. In fact, they're going to tell you your son's going to die. But I laid hands on your son and prayed for him in the name of Jesus. I'm telling you, he's not going to die.

"Now you definitely have a part to play in all this. The Lord is already beginning the healing, but when you go in there, fear will try to attack your thinking. I'm not telling you to go in there and argue. Be polite and listen; they know what they're talking about. But as true as all their information is, God's Word can change all that. I prayed for your boy in the name of Jesus, and he's not going to die. But if you go in there and agree with what they're saying and start speaking that, he will die. You'll negate what's been started by my praying for him. But if every time you get scared or hear a bad report, you thank the Lord for His healing, He will do His part. Have you got it?"

"Yes," Beth said, nodding her head earnestly. "I got it."

"Okay, then. I want you to repeat back to me what I just said you need to do."

Beth dutifully repeated back his instructions.

"Okay," said Dave with approval. "God bless you."

With that, Beth proceeded to the trauma unit.

Beth hurried into reception with our three youngest in tow. "Excuse me, my name is Beth Malarkey. My son William Alexander was just admitted. Can I see my son?"

"No, ma'am. I'm afraid that's not possible right now."

"If he is going to die, I want to say good-bye to him while he's alive. You have to let me see my son!"

+++ Just before I began to speak to Beth, I was suddenly filled with boldness. I told her that the medical staff were going to tell her that Alex would die. However, I had prayed for Alex in the name of Jesus and was confident he would live. Her job was to continue in faith and to thank the Lord continually for healing Alex. I cautioned her that if she gave in to fear and began to say he was going to die, he would. I spent several minutes reminding her that God honors His Word and that Alex was being healed as we spoke. As I walked away, that boldness left and I thought to myself, *What did I do? I'm in trouble now.* However, I didn't speak anything contrary to Alex's being healed; I just continued to thank the Lord.

Dave Knopp, paramedic +++

Despite Beth's pleading, the answer remained a firm no. Sadness and fear turned to frustration and anger. "This is unbelievable! How can they not let me see my son?"

I arrived about ninety minutes later. Beth still had no information about Alex's injuries and had not heard anything concrete about his medical condition. Over the next few hours, we would be told repeatedly that the situation was serious and that the doctors were working on our son. We would not be able to see Alex or get any information about him until he was moved to the ICU.

No Condemnation

When I walked into the hospital, a group of forty people had already gathered to pray and to support us. Some were family members; others were friends from our former and current church families;

still others we didn't even know. Everyone was eager to see that I was okay, at least physically. But when I entered the ICU waiting room, there was only one face I could see in the crowd.

When Beth's eyes met mine, I was flooded again with memories of the hundreds of times she had told me to drive more carefully, to slow down, to pay attention to the road rather than the CD player or the radio. And what about the many times I'd played in the backyard or the family room with Alex and Aaron, laughing and getting crazier by the minute, while Beth stood in the background and asked me if we were being careful? "Just relax," I would always tell her. "Everything's under control. Don't be so overprotective." I was certain these were her thoughts as well.

As I looked into her face, feelings of relief, comfort, grief, and deepest sadness all jumbled together. Renewed waves of shame washed over my tortured heart. She embraced me warmly and lovingly, but deep down I felt I didn't deserve it.

"Beth! Is Alex alive?"

"I think so. I think he's holding on, but I haven't seen him, and they've told me next to nothing."

In that instant the pain squeezed my heart so relentlessly that I collapsed into Beth's arms.

"Oh, Beth," I sobbed as I clung to her for mercy, "please forgive me. Please forgive me! I'm so sorry. I've torn our family apart."

Sobs convulsed my body as grief washed over me in a tide that threatened never to ebb. For a moment, I dared to look into Beth's eyes, bracing myself to take in the condemnation I expected to find. But no. When I looked into her dark eyes, I found only mercy. Beth held me close, covering me with kindness, understanding, and love. No anger, no bitterness, only love.

"Kevin, this could have happened to anyone. It was an accident. Of course you blame yourself. That's just human nature. But when things calm down, you'll realize it's not true. Honey, don't condemn yourself. God won't, and neither will anyone else."

I wasn't sure she was right about any of this, but I felt certain she was being sincere. If Beth was nursing any bitterness or blame toward me for what had happened, I would have been able to sense it in her voice and body language. Her acceptance was a lifeline I desperately needed in that moment.

"So put all that out of your mind," she said. "All I want to know is whether you're all right. Are you sure you don't have any injuries?"

"I'm fine. In fact, I'm a lot better after seeing you. Thanks."

Separate paths had brought Alex, Beth, and me together at the hospital. Yet all we knew was that Alex was barely alive and could slip away at any moment . . .

From Alex
I Watch from the Ceiling

For he will conceal me there when troubles
come; he will hide me in his sanctuary. He will
place me out of reach on a high rock.
PSALM 27:5

When we got to the hospital, I was watching everything that happened from the corner of the emergency room, near the ceiling. Jesus was standing there beside me.

I was not afraid. I felt safe.

The doctors were very busy, working on my body, which by this time was kind of blue. The doctors talked a lot about me, and they didn't have much good to say. They all thought I wouldn't make it. One doctor did say, "He might come back." Mostly though the medical workers were sad and talked a lot about me not surviving.

While everyone was talking about my not living, Jesus said to me that I would survive the accident. He also told me I would breathe on my own after some time had passed.

Then I looked down, and I watched as they attached a steel bolt to my head and said that it was going to hurt. (I heard later that this thing was for measuring the pressure in my brain.) Then they started putting something down my throat, and Jesus moved me into Heaven.

Jesus didn't want me to watch what they did because He didn't want me to remember it later and be scared.

I saw one hundred and fifty pure, white angels with fantastic wings who were all calling my name. If you didn't know they were friendly, they would be really scary. After a while, they all said, "Alex, go back." I did go, but Jesus went with me and held me during my time in the emergency room.

CHAPTER 3

72 HOURS

The doctors had spoken . . . and now we waited on God.

AT LAST A medical assistant led Beth and me to a small conference room. The doctor wanted to speak with us privately. It seemed like hours before he arrived. After we exchanged a few courtesies, he pulled out an X-ray of the injured area at the base of Alex's skull. No medical knowledge was needed to understand the hideous truth the darkened image revealed. Something in me could not accept that this was a picture of Alex's spine. Instinctively, I glanced at the bottom left corner of the sheet: *WILLIAM ALEXANDER MALARKEY*. Those three words were so final, so unambiguous. Any thoughts that the situation might not be all that bad vanished.

The doctor moved across the room to a whiteboard. He sketched a normal spinal column and next to it a picture of Alex's spine. It was easy to see what was wrong. The first vertebra below his skull had been pulled apart from the second and stood at a forty-five-degree angle.

Turning to us, the doctor began, "I must be frank with you. Alex's situation is extremely serious. Injuries involving this spinal alignment virtually always result in death. In point of fact, Alex is presently being kept alive by artificial means. He does have a youthful constitution in his favor, but if he survives, the nature of these injuries will lead to certain outcomes, and it's best to be realistic about them. Given the severity and height of the injury—which is to say its proximity to the base of the brain stem and the trauma sustained by the cerebral cortex—should Alex survive, normal brain function cannot be reasonably expected. Alex will never breathe on his own, and below the neck he will not move on his own. This injury will preclude Alex from swallowing food. He is presently receiving fluids intravenously, but if he survives, we will have to install a gastronomy tube, or G-tube, so he can receive nutrition directly into his stomach. And, finally, if he does survive, he will never be able to speak. I understand these are difficult things to hear. Truly I am sorry."

G-tube, no normal brain function, paralyzed—my eyes fell to the floor, fixed in stunned disbelief. It was all so overwhelming it would have to be sifted through piece by piece, but the doctor had spoken. We would have to deal with it. The information was so horrific and the scale of it so massive that my mind went into numbed acceptance. I'd think more coherently about the details later.

Beth's experience, informed by Dave in the parking lot, was completely different. She wasn't having any of it. I was still looking at the floor when she spoke. Looking directly into the doctor's eyes, she confidently spoke three simple words: "You are wrong."

I inhaled sharply, thoroughly embarrassed. This doctor was the

+++ Trying to take in the scope of Alex's injury was overwhelming. Like looking over the rail at the Grand Canyon, your mind is incapable of grasping the enormity of what you see.

It wasn't explained to us until much later why, medically speaking, it was so unlikely that Alex would survive. He had suffered an internal decapitation—his skull was detached from his spinal column. Skin, muscle, and ligaments were the only things holding his head on his body.

Months later we received an X-ray from a medical professional taken more than an hour after the car accident. The X-ray was of the bottom portion of Alex's skull and the top portion of his spinal cord. The X-ray clearly reveals Alex's vertebrae detached from his head.

Not only was there no mention of this situation to either my wife or me, but there has never been a medical procedure to reattach his skull to his spinal column.

Kevin Malarkey +++

head of a team of top-notch surgeons, all of whom had reviewed Alex's case. We were under the care of one of the best children's trauma units in the country. Who was she to question them? I placed a hand on her arm, trying to get her to stop talking. She needed to sit back and accept reality, as I was doing. Beth pulled away from my touch. She had no intention of backing down.

"Alex is going to be fine. His health will be fully restored, and his story is going to have a national impact, bringing hope to thousands of people."

Okay, I told myself, *she is totally losing it.* I looked at the doctor, confident of what he was thinking, although I have to hand it to him—he listened to Beth with an earnest concern, nodding his head sympathetically. There was not one thought in my mind about Alex helping others. I just wanted my boy to be okay. I wanted my own guilt to dissipate. I wanted my son to regain consciousness long enough for me to ask his forgiveness—a conversation I had already played over in my mind a thousand times since the accident a few hours earlier.

But Beth was just getting started.

"I know you don't believe me, but he *is* going to get better, and I mean completely healthy."

I sat back, helpless to stop the drama. The good doctor continued to nod respectfully. I was sure I could read his mind: *Another poor woman in the grips of an irrational outburst brought on by shocking news she doesn't want to be true . . . seen it thousands of times. It's an opportunity for me to be gracious.*

But I also knew the doctor was wrong, at least about Beth. She never becomes a refugee from reality in a crisis. She's calm and clinical under the most intense pressure. Her words to the doctor were a confident proclamation, not mindless wishful thinking. It was as if she knew something the rest of us hadn't been told. I certainly couldn't see whatever miraculous future she had in view. All I could see was the X-ray and the horrendous prognosis that accompanied it.

"Just wait and see. It will be a medical phenomenon. Alex's story will touch people all across this nation. It will give hope to people who have lost all hope."

Whatever was in her, it wasn't in me. The doctor finished listening and politely excused himself.

+++

What was happening now seemed so surreal. Memories emerged from deep places. I had written a poem for Alex months before he was born, parts of which seemed strangely relevant now:

PRECIOUS CHILD

There is so much I yearn to
Tell you
To teach you
To experience with you
For now, let me share some of my sorrows
You will be exposed to a world
Far different than the womb . . .
Blessed child
What I long to teach you most
Is where you come from
And where you might return . . .

Beth and I trusted God and believed, even before Alex was born, that God had a special life planned for him. Now, in the hush of the hospital, I had to face the end of those plans, at least on earth.

+++

When we returned to the waiting room, even more people had gathered. Some were talking and others were praying. We shared the news we had received from the doctors, and then all the people in the room held hands and began to pray. Many audible prayers were brought to the throne of God in this moment.

In fact, over those first dark days, we turned to God again and again. I don't remember my own prayers or most of the others. But there was one prayer that pierced my darkness the day after the accident.

Our minister, Pastor Brown, had waited for everyone else to pray, and then, following a few moments of silence, he lifted up his voice: "Oh Lord, we know that Alex is with You, even now. The doctors have spoken. And now, Lord, we await Your word on the matter."

Simple and powerful. Yes, what did God have to say on the matter of Alex? Pastor Brown's prayer was a great comfort. Of course, nothing would happen outside of God's supervision. I needed to hang on to that truth. And I did—for a short time.

+++

As Beth and I waited to see Alex that first day, in my mind, I was back at the day of Alex's birth. Another hospital, a day of joy. I was beside Beth, but shielding my eyes from the cesarean surgery—I didn't want to pass out. And then the indescribable moment when he entered our world. . . . The nurse cut the cord, looked over to me, and said, "Would you like to hold William Alexander?"

"Is that his name?"

Beth looked up at me. "Uh, Kevin, that's the name we chose in case we had a boy—remember?" She smiled.

"Oh yeah, that's right," I agreed. "William Alexander, after my dad."

+++

My father, Dr. William Malarkey, an endocrinologist and director of the Clinical Research Center at Ohio State University, was off lecturing somewhere in Europe. Had anyone notified him about the accident? As I sat in the waiting room, surrounded by praying friends and family, a new set of questions came at me like daggers.

If Alex dies, will I go to jail for vehicular homicide?

Did I hurt the people in the other car?

Are we going to lose our house?

Is Beth thinking, "I knew this would happen with Kevin because of all the chances he takes. If he had listened to me, none of this would have happened"?

Is everyone here and at the accident just being kind but really thinking what a rotten person I am—what a pathetic father Alex has?

That first day, fear, doubt, and self-loathing slid in and out of my mind—reasonable, under the circumstances, but also pointless and destructive. I knew these thoughts didn't come from God—they were

---

+++ I was speaking at a medical conference in Europe when the accident occurred. In fact, I was taking pictures of a boy who was a quadriplegic with a respirator in a wheelchair at a park in Paris. At the same time, thousands of miles away in Ohio, unknown to me, my grandson was on a MedFlight and would face a similar outcome. Every time I see a picture of the Eiffel Tower, I am reminded that I had just looked at its lighted outline when I received the phone call about the accident.

Dr. William Malarkey, Kevin's father +++

---

directly from my adversary, the devil. But knowing the truth about these things wasn't enough. I was almost overcome by them. I had to fight against them. I had to reject the false voice and cling to the truth. I began holding on to the only hope I had: *God loves me. God loves Alex. God loves Beth and our other children.* God's peace was there, available for me, but I had to receive it by rejecting the Accuser and listening to the Voice of Truth. *I* will *listen to the Voice of Truth.*

+++

Another memory came to me . . . a happy one. Alex was just a few days old, and to get him off to a proper start, I held him up to see Ohio Stadium.

"Hey, buddy," I said, holding him face out, "that's where the Buckeyes play football!"

Yes, I had planned this initiation rite well in advance. On check-in to the birthing center, just before Alex's delivery, I had managed to secure the hospital room that afforded the best view of the stadium. Now, sitting in the hospital waiting room, I wondered, *Why am I thinking about this now?*

+++

At last a hospital worker arrived to lead us to Alex's room. We were about to go into a very different hospital room from the one of my memory. I had never before been in an intensive care unit. Walking down the hall, I thought how strange it was that none of the rooms had doors. Only loosely hanging, shabby-looking drapes separated us from the many families and the trauma that engulfed them. For all their plainness, those drapes wielded tremendous power to shield passersby from the pain within each room. The hollow gaze of hopeless anguish flooded through the doorways with open drapes. The children I saw looked so sick, so distressed. Alex would look much different, I assured myself, much better.

When we rounded the corner and stepped into Alex's room, I took a sharp breath. The scene was overwhelming. It was as if we had stepped into the command center in some diabolical war. Alex lay flaccid, eyes closed, on a bed in the center of the room. He was completely surrounded by a riot of monitors, wires, tubes, and endless medical paraphernalia. A ventilator conspicuously pumped air into his lungs.

Yet other than the obvious trauma points and the tubes running in and out of his body, he looked fairly normal, at least at first glance. Garish evidence of the accident was mercifully spare, just a few small scrapes and one deep gash held together by stitches.

A moment later, though, the icy fingers of fear once again encircled my heart—he looked . . . lifeless. How do you describe what it means to be a parent and to stand, helpless, over the broken body of your child? Yet in that very moment, something deep inside me believed Alex would survive—in what condition I dared not think. But from that moment on, an assurance that he would live took root, never to be dislodged.

Please, God, help our son.

+++

I remembered praying with Alex as he received Jesus as his Savior a few years before. He was so young, yet so sincere. What an awesome privilege! Alex knew he wanted to go to Heaven someday, and he grasped that he could not go simply by "being a good boy." Heaven could not be earned like other things. Alex knew he needed someone else to pay the price for his sin—the wrong things he would do in his life—so that he could accept the gift of going to Heaven and being with God.

I have to admit, I did wonder about the sincerity of his faith. What can a child understand about the depths of faith at this age? Surely kids only mindlessly repeat the words and ideas adults feed them, without really understanding the truth.

A few weeks after Alex prayed to invite Jesus into his life, I put his faith to the test.

"Alex, does Jesus live in your heart?"

"No, Daddy."

My heart sank. There it was, I thought. His prayer had been meaningless . . . but then Alex continued, "Jesus died for my sins, but He doesn't live in my heart—He wouldn't fit. The Holy Spirit is in my heart now."

So Alex did understand—Jesus had died for his sins and left the Holy Spirit as His Comforter and Counselor. I learned my lesson then and there: a young child is able to grasp the things God wants him to know.

+++

Suddenly my consciousness was jerked back into the present. There was my precious son, lying in front of me. I took assurance from the fact that the Holy Spirit would be with Alex forever, but would God allow *me* to be with Alex again in this world?

What else was there to do but to cry out to God for mercy? We didn't know it then, but even the best doctors are quick to admit they don't understand these situations very well. I could do nothing but beg God for help.

Oh God, please forgive me for what I have done. Please let me apologize to Alex. Please protect him. Please comfort him. Please be his heavenly Father because his earthly father is completely helpless. I give You my son. I let go of him. He is Yours. Please help him from the top of his head to the bottom of his feet. I trust You, God. In Jesus' name, amen.

Somehow in God's mercy, my spirit was bathed in a new sense of calm at the end of that prayer. Had some kind of spiritual transfer occurred? My theology already settled the matter of God's being in complete control of the situation. God had already wrapped His arms around Alex, but had something fundamentally changed in Heaven because of my prayer to completely release Alex to God . . . to let go of what I couldn't hold on to anyway? Somehow, it seemed so.

Beth and I stayed and looked on our son in silence. How long, I don't know. In the quietness, I slipped my arm around her, probably more for my comfort than for hers. The coma took Alex someplace we couldn't reach him. I stared, wondering as my heart ached for my broken son. *Little buddy, are you lonely? Are you scared? Do you want me to hold you? How desperately I want to hold you.*

+++

I remembered how much Alex had loved church. We belonged to a casual-dress church. For the most part, people dressed comfortably, and kids wore school clothing. Not Alex. He decided he wanted to wear a suit to church. Even with Daddy in khakis and a dress shirt, even with a pastor who almost never wore a suit, Alex wanted to wear a suit. He has never been a go-along-with-the-crowd type. He never wore a suit anywhere else. He wanted to dress up for God.

And then I thought about another side of Alex—the one that spent as much time outdoors as possible. I remembered one day how deeply satisfied he looked as he walked barefoot in the back garden, crunching autumn leaves with his toes. "Daddy," he asked, "don't you just love the sound of the leaves under your feet?"

+++

At some point during our first evening at the hospital, we were ushered into a room designated for parents whose kids were in the ICU. Our other three children had gone to stay with some of our friends, and we soon found ourselves alone in bed, staring at the ceiling in silence. What had just happened to our lives? What would tomorrow bring? Would Alex make it through the night? Where was he, really? The accident had traumatized his body. The coma had taken him far away. When would he come back? *Would* he come back?

Oh God, we need You now . . .

In a fit of exhaustion, we slept.

+++

For the first week, Beth and I never even left the hospital; we weren't interested in being anywhere else. At the same time, support came flowing in. The first group to assemble for help was made up of friends, family, and our church family, led by Pastor Brown. But soon the exponentially growing number of men and women around Alex and our family could only be described as an army.

Our children were with us virtually the entire time, but on those occasions when they weren't, they were warmly loved and nurtured by friends or family. For instance, a few women took turns rocking, feeding, and changing our newborn whenever Beth couldn't be with him. Someone organized the delivery of all our meals. Someone else organized the bringing of fresh clothes and the laundering of dirty clothes, as well as providing any personal items we needed. Errands were handled by someone else. So much food began appearing that there was a buffet line in the ICU waiting room at one point. It remained for days as people removed and replaced covered dishes as necessary. Get-well cards bearing notes, prayers, and Scripture verses flowed in until every square inch of Alex's room was papered over with them. The doctors and nurses were dumbfounded and often commented that they had never seen such an outpouring of love.

A steady stream of godly men—elders, deacons, pastors, and lay leaders—along with many godly women arrived from every corner of the state. Common were the stories of people who "felt God tugging at their hearts to come." One pastor drove two hours just to visit Alex. Since he arrived after visiting hours and wasn't on the pre-arranged schedule, the hospital denied him admittance to Alex's room. Undaunted, he drove home, only to turn around the next morning and drive back, spending most of the day praying over Alex. During those first few critical days, many local youth groups came as well, singing praise and worship songs in Alex's room. At any given time, there were never fewer than five people in Alex's room during visiting hours.

Within a short time, there were so many visitors that someone organized a visiting schedule to accommodate them all. Even more important, someone organized a night-watch prayer vigil in Alex's room. Every two hours, someone was praying over Alex throughout the night—every night, for months. Many of these saints we never met. They were there serving God in obscurity, for His glory.

The ministry to Alex and our family engendered so much activity that the hospital had to organize itself, too, in order to handle all the traffic. Hospital staff printed up stacks of "Alex" passes with his name and room number. They told us that Alex typically had more visitors than the rest of the ICU patients combined, a situation the saints soon endeavored to remedy.

The prayer/visiting/blessing ministry that started with Alex soon fanned out to the other families in the ICU. In this God reserved a special blessing for Beth and me. We had been completely absorbed with Alex and his care—understandable, yes, but when we joined those who came to minister to Alex and went from room to room in the ICU to comfort others and to pray with them, God did something in our hearts. These firsthand encounters with other families experiencing deep trials were a poignant reminder in the midst of our own sorrow that there were many other people suffering just as much as we were. It helped us gain perspective, helped us to turn outward and see in a new light the blessings God was bestowing so abundantly on us.

If you were looking for good food and good Christian fellowship during that mid-November, there was no better place than Children's Hospital and the ministry that grew up around Alex. We could never begin to appropriately thank the thousands who blessed us with their selfless giving. If there ever was a time when the church enveloped needy souls in arms of love, we experienced it.

Oh, and one more thing. That stack of unpaid bills overflowing my bill basket back home, which I had fretted so much about prior to the accident? It disappeared. I never got the chance to tape that God Will Provide sign on the side of it. A wonderful man whom I have always held in the highest regard made a quiet trip out to our empty house during that first week we were in the hospital. He took the entire basket and paid every bill to the last penny—an immense sum. But these things have a way of getting out. *Thank you, God, for Your beautiful saints.*

Two by Two

On the third day following the accident, there was an unexpected development. A nurse approached me and asked, "Mr. Malarkey, may I have a word with you in private?"

"Sure."

We walked into the hall, and she began to speak, hesitated, and began again. "Uh, Mr. Malarkey . . . I know you'll understand—I'm sure you'll agree—from now on, we need to limit Alex's visitors to no more than two people in his room at a time."

"I certainly do understand, but I hope this didn't come about because our friends have abused our visiting privileges. If so, I would like to apologize for—"

"Oh, no, sir! That's not it at all, I . . . I promise," she replied in haste. "Not that the numbers haven't been overwhelming. But everyone has been *very* respectful of the hospital rules."

"Oh, that's good to hear. But then why the rule change?"

"Well," she hesitated, searching for words with a side-glance, "it's not a change, really—it's just, well, a guideline we should be following."

I nodded, but my mind raced to understand. At that very moment, there were twenty people on the waiting list in the lobby ready to go in, five at a time, to pray for Alex—just like the previous seventy-two hours. I rarely take things at face value, and this wasn't making sense to me. Why was this policy so important today, if not yesterday or the day before? Clearly there was something she didn't want to tell me. Then the light went on.

"The doctors just figured out that Alex is going to live, didn't they?"

The nurse nodded, a little sheepishly, and then leaned in, assuming a confidential tone. "I've worked on this unit for twelve years. I have *never* seen a child survive the kind of injury your child sustained—*never.*"

Seventy-two hours had been the time frame the medical staff had stressed. They'd been watching the clock. The unit workers had not expected Alex to cross over into this day with a beating heart.

My heart leaped for joy as I hurried back to the lobby, gathered everyone there, and issued the new rule and explained its reason. A cheer went up, and everyone praised God. The visitors list was reorganized for groups of two. Once there, they could pray for as long as they felt the need—then they had to give their place to someone else. To help accommodate the steady stream of people, we agreed there would be no conversation in the room other than with God. Alex would have two people praying beside his bed at all times.

+++

As I sat by Alex one day that week, another memory surfaced. Just a few months before, Alex had actually caught air when riding on a local BMX course. He and I were at the top of the biggest hill on the course when I turned my head to see where Aaron had gone. In that instant,

Alex launched down the giant hill. Although my emotions were doing a bungee jump as I watched him gain enormous speed, he actually stuck the landing! He had also learned how to do a flip one day on a friend's trampoline. A few weeks later he was at the perfect location to execute the flip he had been practicing—the side of a swimming pool! He scared us to death, but again nailed the landing. Before the accident, Alex could be socially shy and sometimes clingy with his mommy and daddy; when it came to physical activities, however, he was fearless.

Now as I sat by my boy's bedside, I couldn't help but wonder, What would happen to him now? Would he ever have a chance to act with such fearlessness again?

+++

When Alex moves again, we are going to have a bike race.

Gracie Malarkey, Alex's sister

From Alex

Inside the Gates

I knew you before I formed you in your mother's womb. Before you were born I set you apart and appointed you as my prophet to the nations.

JEREMIAH 1:5

Heaven is not the next world; it is now.

Heaven is not up in the sky; it is everywhere and nowhere.

Heaven is a place that is not a place. It's eternal. All other places end.

Heaven is a time with no past, present, or future . . . it is always now.

When I was in the car, I tried to move my legs. I realized that they would not move. I went through a light and I heard music.

Then I was in the presence of God. He had a body that was like a human body, but it was a lot bigger. I could only see up to His neck because, like the Bible says, nobody is allowed to see God's face or that person will die. He had on a white robe that was very bright. I looked down at my legs, and I could move them again.

Even right now as I tell you this, I feel in my heart just like I did when it happened.

Everything was perfect.

My daddy told me about a man who wrote about spending time in Heaven. He had a bad car accident like me, and he went to Heaven and heard incredible music and saw glorious colors—like me. But this man saw people he had met in life who had talked to him about Jesus. When I was in Heaven right after the accident, I didn't see any people, only God, Jesus, and angels.

But when I heard the story, I told my daddy that this man was not in Heaven.

My daddy was surprised. Daddy said that this man was a pastor and that he believed him. I told Daddy that the man's story was true; it's just that, technically (one of my new favorite words), the man stayed outside the gates of Heaven. Then my daddy told me that's what the man says in the book! I asked Daddy, "He didn't see God or any angels, did he?" Daddy said that's what the man said in his book. I also told Daddy he wasn't there very long. Daddy said that was true; he was there only about an hour and a half. Daddy asked me how I knew that. It's because he didn't get to see much of the good stuff, I told him. All of the heavenly beings are inside the gate. God must have wanted him back to earth right away.

When I went to Heaven, I arrived on the inside of the gate. I was with heavenly beings, but the other people who came to Heaven were all on the outside of the gate.

The gate is really tall, and it's white. It is very shiny, and it looks like it has scales like a fish.

I think of the things on the outside of the gate as an outer Heaven. I was in the inner Heaven, and everything is brighter and more intense on the inside of the gate.

There is a hole in outer Heaven. That hole goes to hell.

Later, my daddy asked me to tell him about other differences between the inside and outside of the gate, but I had to tell him that I am not allowed to share some things. God told me not to. I don't know why; it's just what He said. I asked my daddy if he was mad about this, but he just hugged me and told me that obeying God is more important than anything.

But I can say that inside the gate is the place God has prepared for us. It is brighter and more colorful. It is impossible to describe . . . it's glorious!

The outside of the gates is like a waiting room. Things don't move on the outside like they do on the inside. They move, but it's not the same. I can't describe it.

That other man who spent time in Heaven is right: the

music is beautiful. He said it was like many songs at the same time—but sounding like one song. I didn't think it was a bunch of songs at the same time, just very intense. It's beautiful. I really liked the harps inside the gates. The music is nothing like music here. It is perfect!

Perfect is my favorite word for describing Heaven.

CHAPTER 4

AN ARMY GATHERS

The truth was that Alex's story had grown bigger than our family, bigger than our church, bigger than even our local community. People sensed that this was Heaven's business.

THREE DAYS AFTER the accident, I woke up and made my way to the shower. I had slept fitfully the night before. It felt good to let the steaming water cascade down my face as I wondered, Was Alex experiencing something like sleep? What was happening to him? Where was he? He had seen his way through the first three days . . . but would he remain asleep forever?

Medically speaking, there were so many unanswered questions, so many uncertainties. Beth and I would have given anything just to do something practical for Alex to improve his chances. The most we could do, however, was to pray, and we had to remind ourselves that this was a significant contribution.

But we felt there was something else we could do: we could get the word out to everyone who believed in the power of prayer and who might agree to intercede for Alex before God.

People had been calling the hospital and pouring into the hallways since the moment visiting hours began—we'd never dreamed that we had so many true friends and loved ones and would make so many new friends besides. But we wanted to spread the word far and wide, to Columbus, to Ohio, and to the uttermost parts of the earth, if possible, so that prayer warriors everywhere would take up Alex's cause. We'd heard stories of miracles that happened when God's people were diligent in taking their requests before the Lord. We simply weren't prepared, however, for the depth of the encounters we would soon be having in prayer as we became surrounded by a group of saints we called Alex's Army.

"Nice" Christians or Prayer Warriors?

How often do we hear people described as "nice"?

But is that really what our faith is all about? Isn't it possible to appear to be a pleasant person, with a smiling face, saying all the right words to give the impression that one is close to God? Isn't it revealing that Jesus, the apostle Paul, and all of the great saints of the Bible were *never* described as nice?

God had taken care of where He placed us—not among your average "nice" people, but among true men and women of God, soldiers of the Cross who were ready to mobilize. These were people who understood spiritual warfare in ways the vast majority of us never recognize.

What's all the more amazing is that these were *practical* people as well. Some

+++

I have a strong faith, but I am a weak man. Please pray that God continually refreshes me and that I not fall prey to the fiery darts of the evil one.

PrayforAlex.com
post by Kevin Malarkey
on December 10, 2004

served God with their hearts, others with their hands, but the people around us excelled in both faith *and* works. As Alex lay there in a coma and as we stood watching, shocked and numb—with our other children needing us—God used the ministry of prayer-centric people to sustain us and to carry on the fight for Alex's recovery.

Our lives were quickly becoming intertwined with those of prayer warriors in ways that we'll never forget as long as we live. One of them had a most unusual name.

Hillbilly Graham

Neither *Hillbilly* nor *Graham* appeared on his birth certificate. He had the distinction of a double nickname. The first came about because of his entertaining country accent, the second because of his remarkable passion for introducing people to the Lord—a genuine "hillbilly" version of Billy Graham. What made this man's nicknames even more amusing was that he was actually a successful dentist who resided in one of the affluent suburbs of Columbus.

Knowing Hillbilly's spiritual wisdom, I was excited to see him walk into Alex's room during our first full day in the hospital. Hillbilly visited with us for a few minutes and quickly became a comforting presence, describing times of sickness and trouble in his own family and explaining how prayer had made the difference—how it could do the same for our Alex.

A question had been forming in my mind, and it occurred to me that Hillbilly might be just the person to answer it. But it was the kind of question I wanted to phrase very carefully.

"Hillbilly, can I ask you something?" I offered tentatively. "I'm a little reluctant to say it, because I don't want you to get the wrong idea."

"Don't worry 'bout that!" said Hillbilly in his trademark drawl. "What's on your mind, Kevin?"

"Well, you see, since Alex was very little, I've had this strong feeling that someday he might be a pastor. You know, I've watched him closely, and I've known he was spiritually sensitive and special in so many ways. And I just began believing that someday he would feel a call to the ministry."

My eyes moved down to take in the image of my little boy who had engendered such lofty ideas, which now seemed refuted by all the machines, tubes, and IVs running chaotically in every direction. "Then, well, since the accident, I've started to wonder if it could be the devil behind this whole thing—I mean, causing the accident. Because if I were the devil and I spotted this child who had great potential to serve God, I'd want to cut him off at the pass, right?"

Hillbilly began to nod and smile as if he knew exactly what I was saying.

"Now don't get me wrong," I added quickly. "I'm not passing off responsibility for what I did. It was *me* behind the wheel, not the devil. I've never been the kind to say 'the devil made me do it' whenever I spill a glass of milk, and I'm *not* trying to pass off the blame on some invisible—"

Hillbilly threw his head back and burst out laughing. His big hand came down hard on my shoulder, *smack!*

"Bless your heart, man. I'm right there with ya. What you want to know is—did the devil want to kill your son? And I say, 'Ya *think?*'"

Then he waved a hand across the room, where people were praying. He continued, "Yes *sir*, I believe the devil tried to kill your son—

but you know what? As usual, all he accomplished was to stir up a hornet's nest!"

I stopped, looked, and listened to the hushed murmur of praying voices that filled the room like soft music. Hillbilly was exactly right. The only thing the devil had accomplished was to mobilize the saints to turn to God. How quickly they had organized to spread the love of Christ by meeting our needs and serving as a major witness to everyone who came in the doors of Children's. I suddenly felt buoyed by an incredible power.

"The Spirit who lives in you," wrote the apostle John, "is greater than the spirit who lives in the world" (1 John 4:4). Since I had watched the helicopter bear my son away, I had felt totally weak and helpless. Now I was realizing, in a very practical way, that there are other ways to see things. You can choose to view life as an impersonal machine that provides no user's manual, or you can see it as a spiritual battle in progress, in which a prayer army can make a real difference.

Ours was already on the front line, and I was beginning to gain courage from their presence.

As we continued to discuss these things, someone near me suggested that we leave Alex's room and adjourn to an empty one across the hall. I figured we were doing this out of consideration for the people trying to pray. But as soon as we got there, Hillbilly pushed me down into a chair. Then he gathered everyone in a circle around me. This was for me! It was the last thing I was expecting, and I felt a little awkward. But all I could do was go with the flow. Everyone present laid hands on me while Hillbilly knelt at my feet. He asked me to fully extend my legs. Then he held my feet in the air and began praying.

"Lord God," he said, "we need Your wisdom right now so that we might understand how to pray and what to ask for. Use us as vessels for Your healing power." The others whispered their prayerful affirmation. "We are here for Alex, dear Lord," he continued, "but now we lift his father, Kevin, before You. He is a victim of this accident too. Heal him in every way, mind and body. You are the Great Physician; place Your healing hand upon him, we pray, in Jesus' name."

Hillbilly Graham finished praying, placed my feet back on the floor, and said, "You're done."

"I beg your pardon?" I asked.

"You're going to have no physical problems from that wreck," he said. "God is strengthening you so you can be strong for your family."

The Art of Prayer

I did have some soreness from the accident. I still limped a little and had that sharp pain in my neck when I turned my head just so. It's typical to have lingering physical problems, which can last for years, from the kind of contortions a body goes through in an accident like ours. The soreness and pain in my neck didn't vanish immediately, but an amazing thing did happen: following Hillbilly's prayer—and to this day—I have never needed any medication or medical help of any kind for those injuries and have no residual or recurring problems.

I looked around me at those faithful friends who were gently gripping my arms and shoulders, asking God to intervene for my health. Just the day before I'd been wondering, *What do these people really think about me?* Here was what they thought: they loved me and wanted God's best for me.

I felt ashamed for having doubted them. How often did I do others the injustice of assuming the worst about them? I still had my own guilt to contend with, but it was such a relief to know there were brothers and sisters in Christ who had my back, who wouldn't judge me, and who would pray for me when it was so very difficult to pray for myself. The love they showed filled me with a fresh energy to pray for Alex.

Hillbilly Graham was not finished, however, and he had a question for everyone. "Is there anyone here who has any unconfessed sin in their hearts? We can't approach God effectively when hiding sin in our lives. He won't hear us. The only thing we accomplish when we pray without examining ourselves is to obstruct prayer. We need to prepare our hearts, so if there is anyone here who needs to get right with God, now is a good time to take care of it. Let's bring those sins before God and receive the forgiveness He offers. Let's be as pure as we possibly can before we take up the huge task of praying for this little boy. Everyone take a moment and reflect silently. First John 1:9 says, 'If we confess our sins to him, he is faithful and just to forgive us our sins and to cleanse us from all wickedness.' Let's confess before God and then come together in prayer for Alex."

There were many incredible prayer sessions during this period, but this one and Pastor Brown's in the waiting room the night before truly stand out. There was a palpable feeling of the presence of God among us.

In prayer, we reiterated that the doctors had spoken and that we wanted God to have His say. We prayed for Alex's brain and skull, we prayed for his breathing, for the healing of his spine, and finally that the doorway to death would be locked shut for him. We knew that

Heaven awaited him someday, but we believed that God had more for him to do in this world. As usual, Hillbilly led the charge.

There was a midweek church service a week or two later, and the congregation was again praying for Alex while we kept our vigil at the hospital. Hillbilly felt something touch his soul during that prayer, and he began to weep uncontrollably. When I heard about it, I gave him a phone call.

"What is happening, Hillbilly?" I asked. "What made you cry?"

"I had an amazing sensation. Kevin, things are happening in Heaven that concern Alex. The Spirit of God is moving. I could feel it as we prayed together, and I just felt overcome with emotion."

Science and Sovereignty

The testimony of science said that Alex was unconscious and that he wasn't even breathing on his own—he was physically incapable of movement. As far as the world knew, Alex lay still and quiet in a coma. The doctors felt there was very little hope for his survival. And even if Alex's body did continue to hang on, there was the question of his mental function. There had been traumatic injury to his brain, and we were told that the sweet six-year-old boy we had known would never speak to us again.

But Alex's testimony is that he was as wide-awake and attentive as Beth, the other children, or me. As you've already read, he has a detailed memory of how the accident played out. He can remember the men removing him from the car and saying that he was a brave boy. He recalls seeing me get into the ambulance, after the helicopter had flown away—yet he doesn't remember the helicopter ride, in which he actually participated.

How can we explain these things? Alex certainly knows what he saw, heard, and felt; he has never wavered on any of the details. He offers his memories, and it's up to the rest of us to draw our own conclusions. It seems to me, on hearing his account, that God allowed my son to see all the events at the accident scene. Then Alex's spirit was called deeper into Heaven for the remarkable events that were to transpire there.

Science presented us with relentless and devastating facts: a near brain–spinal cord separation, a broken pelvis, and traumatic brain injury. Furthermore, the injury to his spinal cord was at the C1-C2 cervical vertebrae level—so high that the spinal cord and brain constituted one massive injury field. That in itself is generally enough to cause death. In addition, there was still the possibility of further damage. In the first days following the accident, Alex's doctors were particularly concerned that swelling in the brain might occur, and with it, increased pressure inside the skull. The surgeons connected a monitor to Alex's brain to get a reading on his intracranial pressure. The doctors explained this to me, as did Alex, who later told me how it appeared from his vantage point and described the pain it had caused him.

There are scientific facts, and there is God's sovereignty. Surrounded by prayer warriors, I was reminded of the truth that God is not controlled by what we know. I was determined to pour out my heart to God in hopes that the predictions of the

+++

The vertebrae were completely detached. The tendon sheath around the spinal column was severed near the base of his brain. The injury was so severe and so high on the spinal column, it is simply incredible that Alex survived.

Dr. Raymond Onders,
Christopher Reeve's and
Alex's doctor

medical community would be confounded. I would soon be joined by more people than I could ever have imagined.

ICU, a House of Prayer

I've never been in such a prayer-filled environment as during the time of Alex's coma. With so many good people lifting up our son and interceding for other children in the ICU and needy people identified by our Web site, the hospital's ICU became holy ground.

The group supporting Alex began to be a major presence at the hospital. Like the first light of dawn breaking over the horizon and bathing everything in light, people who had come to minister were everywhere.

Our section of the hospital began to look and feel more and more like church. Some people moved their small-group Bible studies from their living rooms to the ICU. Others came to visit and pray every day over a period of weeks. It was strange that my son's tragedy could create such joyful fellowship, unity, and ministry. But God does work in mysterious ways.

Sometimes God revealed His plans through someone who had come to pray for Alex. One time while my friend Jay stood with me beside Alex's bed, he gave me a nervous look and began, "I have something to share with you."

"Sure." I smiled. "What's that?"

"Last night I was sitting at home thinking about Alex," he said. "I began to pray for him, and God suddenly laid something on my heart. Kevin, I realized with absolute certainty that Alex would be fully healed."

I looked into his face, not knowing what to say. Jay wasn't the kind of person known for dramatic, supernatural proclamations—I'd never before heard anything like that from him.

I placed my hand on his shoulder and nodded in an effort to appear as if I embraced what he was saying. But he wasn't finished. With emotion rising in his voice, he continued. "When I was younger, I received a phone call from the hospital one evening. The doctor said my father was ill, but he assured me it was nothing life threatening. I don't know why, but deep down I just didn't believe him. Somehow I knew my father was going to die. Don't ask me how or why—I just knew. I could take you to that house and show you exactly where I was standing when it happened. Soon after I hung up the phone, my father died. I felt grief but was not surprised at all. I *knew* it was going to happen. Do you understand?"

"Wow," I said, still at a loss for what to say.

"From that time to this," he continued, "nothing like that has happened to me again. That is, until last night, when it suddenly came to me that Alex is going to be fully healed."

I thought a lot about what Jay had said. It was similar to what Dave, who had been on the helicopter with Alex, had told Beth. Then there was Beth herself, who had blurted out a kind of prognosis prophecy about Alex, including that his story would bless people across the nation. There had been any number of statements or stories from people that had been out of the ordinary during this short period. They all had in common a consistent message of hope and healing for Alex.

I wanted to believe. I wanted it all to be true, but I was a long way from receiving it.

A few days later, Jay rejoined us at the hospital and took me aside again. I was eager to hear what he might say this time. But

Jay seemed much less comfortable than he had been on the last occasion—almost pained.

"I don't want to tell you this," he said.

"But I hope you will," I replied.

After an anguished silence, Jay took a deep breath and finally began.

"Kevin," he said, "I know you've always believed that Alex was destined to be a pastor. I'm here to tell you that it's going to be bigger than that. He's going to be more like Billy Graham."

Again, it struck me as odd for this particular friend to say such startling things. I'm sure he could see that my eyes were wide open. Like many people, I tend to place Billy Graham on a pedestal. There are Christians; then there is *Billy Graham*.

"But his impact will be different," my friend continued. "Billy Graham's ministry was to teach people how to have a personal relationship with God through Jesus Christ. Alex is going to emerge from his coma, and his ministry will be to show people *what God is like*. But just like Dr. Graham, your son will have an impact across the world."

I stared at him with several half-formed words passing over my lips but didn't make a sound. *Showing people the world over what God is like? That's what Alex is going to do?* It's not that I was opposed to the idea, but the incongruity of it all made it impossible for me to put my thoughts into words.

My friend came to the rescue. "I told you I didn't want to tell you. It makes me as uncomfortable as you seem to be. It sounds a little crazy, Kevin, I know, and you probably think I'm nuts. But I *know* it. I know in my heart it's true, just like I know the sun is shining today—the same way I knew I was supposed to be faithful and give you this message even though I didn't want to."

These heady days continued with repeated confirmations about Alex's coming ministry. But there he was, still in a coma, still breathing only because a machine was pushing air into his lungs, his life hanging in the balance from day to day. It would be months before we saw all the groundwork God had already laid for the fulfillment of His purposes.

The praying continued. Alex's Army continued to wage battle, and new recruits joined the front line every day.

Alex Online

From the beginning, we wanted to get the word out so that people could pray for Alex. But how could we keep people updated so they would know specifically how to pray? Naturally, the Internet was the way to go. The hospital provided a link on its own Web site to CaringBridge, a nonprofit organization that provides free Web sites to connect family and friends during serious health situations. But for Alex, we wanted a place on the Web that was more personal and that would be designed to bring glory and honor to God.

John Sullivan, a family friend, knew exactly what to do. John is a Web designer, and he took it upon himself to build a site called PrayforAlex.com. He registered the domain, got pictures from us, and put together a beautiful Web site that allowed people to stay up-to-the-minute on Alex's ongoing story, leave messages for us, and encourage their friends to pray for Alex.

When the site first went live, we had a section called Alex Updates, where we frequently provided new information. John was able to show us how thousands of people were beginning their day by logging on to our site, getting the news on Alex, and praying accordingly. The section for prayer requests was only about Alex's needs in the beginning, but before long it became a clearinghouse for the needs of others, too. People would post requests, and "Alex's Army" would take up their causes as well. Then there was a feedback feature on the site, which allowed people to communicate with our family. I remembered back to the year before the accident, when Alex and I had started the "Daddy and Alex Prayer Journal." We'd write down prayer requests for others and ourselves and circle the request when we felt God had answered a prayer. Now we had what amounted to an online version of that journal—for Alex.

PrayforAlex.com couldn't have been a bigger success. It was accessed more than one million times during its first six months alone. Most of our family messages were read by one thousand visitors or more. We added a Global Prayer Group section that demonstrated, within just a few days, that our son had countless prayer partners all across the United States and, in a very short time, from around the world, including Australia, Hong Kong, Germany, South Africa, England, Iraq, Costa Rica, Canada, Afghanistan, and Honduras. The Alex's Army prayer initiative had truly become an international movement. Many of these correspondents reported that their entire churches were praying for Alex.

We began to hear stories of people waking up at the same time each night for weeks or months, feeling a strong leading of the Holy Spirit to pray for Alex. It was not uncommon to hear of twenty or more individuals, spread across the globe, all praying for Alex at the same time. Hearing these reports filled our hearts with the fresh wind of encouragement, revealing that God was up to something magnificent. Knowing that God was moving in the hearts of people everywhere made our hopes soar.

The site had begun simply as a useful tool. What it became was a worldwide forum for God's work, ministering to us as well as to people we're likely never to know. It reminded us again that God's work is not limited, isolated, or performed in some kind of spiritual vacuum. Everything He does is interconnected, so that when He blesses one person there is a ripple effect of blessings at large. The sad or tragic things, too, become raw material for the demonstration of His power.

Indeed, all things really do work together for our good when we know God.

We dared to face the reality that something as devastating as the automobile accident and Alex's horrific injuries could actually become an amazing blessing in the hands of the Lord. This didn't mean we were happy about what had happened to our boy or that we would want it to happen to anyone else. But we knew that, as

---

+++ The question I get asked so much is, "Where is God, and how is God in the midst of suffering?" If you ever doubt God is there, remember this: He knew the pain we'd be assaulted with. He supplied His hands, His body, His love, and His compassion in the way He knew He could minister to us and sustain us.

There was an orchestration of people 24-7, sitting with and praying over Alex. People came to us and said, "You don't know me, but I woke up at three o'clock in the morning and was compelled to pray for your son." The prime target of the enemy is the nighttime, when our minds and physical bodies are trying to rest. But the Spirit never sleeps.

Beth Malarkey, Alex's mom +++

Corrie ten Boom used to say, "There is no pit so deep that God's love is not deeper still." I was learning to trust more deeply in God than I ever had . . . to accept the bitter and sweet of His plan . . . to open myself to the prayers and insights of fellow believers . . . to accept that something beautiful was happening beyond my powers of control or comprehension.

What about Alex? Was he really as unresponsive as he looked? Was he aware of God's presence? What was he learning . . . experiencing . . . ?

From Alex

Heaven and Earth

We know that all creation has been groaning as in the pains of childbirth right up to the present time.

ROMANS 8:22

God created the earth to be a perfect place for us, and we've messed it up.

Heaven is the perfect place for His children, and it has stayed that way.

Heaven is what this world was supposed to be.

Lots of things in Heaven are similar to things here on earth. There are trees and fields of grass, lakes and rivers, and many other parts of the earth that we know.

It's just that in Heaven, every last detail is perfect.

Maybe you will see a sunset and think that it is the most

beautiful thing there could be. Or you see a mountaintop with snow on it. And you think—that's perfect!

But I think it is impossible to describe what I really want to tell you—these things you are seeing are not perfect! They are warped compared to Heaven.

Sin has warped the earth, and even the colors here are less bright than in Heaven.

So there are lakes and other natural things in Heaven, but they aren't like our lakes. There are also things in Heaven that we don't have here on earth.

I think my daddy gets frustrated sometimes because I use words like *perfect*, *glorious*, or *beyond* over and over. I have to. Heaven is just not like earth.

CHAPTER 5

MIRACLES, MESSES, AND MORE MIRACLES

My son couldn't function in the physical world,
but it was difficult for me to function in the
spiritual world. Who had the greater disability?

THE SENSE OF God's presence was becoming more palpable than I had ever known. Miracles were happening to Alex—though we did not yet know it. What we did know was the miracle of Christian fellowship and through it the sense that God was at work in ways that were both mysterious and real.

But I wouldn't want you to think that Beth and I are miraculous people. After all, this book is a work of nonfiction. In the first few months following the accident, as we were being lifted up into God's presence, we were also feeling frayed at the edges, becoming tense, frustrated, despairing, and, sadly, even nasty to each other. I don't want to write these facts off as normal for people under the kind of stress we were under, but I do want to be honest. Often we were far from behaving in the way Christ envisions for His people—that is the truth, no matter how else I would wish it to be.

Thank God, there is another truth: God continued to be faithful to us in the midst of our messes.

+++ I'd read books on spiritual warfare and obviously read about it in Scripture. I knew what it was to war, but the Malarkey family gave me a motion picture of what spiritual warfare looks like. They were a family at the edge more than once, but by the grace of God they never went over the edge. I really believe that hell brought its best against the Malarkey family, and God just kept bringing them back. Kevin and Beth know what it is to endure and be faithful.

Pastor Gary Brown,
the Malarkeys' pastor at the time of the accident +++

It is one thing to read the Scriptures and affirm their truth. But until you are in the trenches of trial, until you are faced with life circumstances that test your faith, until you are pressed to the absolute limit of your physical and emotional capacity, until you face the unrelenting stress of ongoing trauma, you never really know how you'll respond to what you may have embraced so easily during a comfortable Bible study.

Our Marriage Takes a Battering

My relationship with Beth was stretched to the breaking point. We are told in Scripture to keep our eyes on Jesus, even in the midst of a raging storm. When Beth and I failed to do that, when we gave ourselves over to the flesh, the intensity of our lives made even the smallest issues loom larger than a mountain. I would lose my temper in a discussion about child care, for instance, or over what we were going to do for dinner. It sounds foolish, I know, but at times we were each so caught up with our own pain, fears, and physical exhaustion that we gave full vent to our baser selves. Beth and I have to be honest and admit that our relationship suffered great trauma, not only during Alex's first weeks in the hospital, but also for years after the accident.

I knew all the Bible verses written especially for me, such as "Husbands, . . . love your wives, just as Christ loved the church." And Beth knew all the Bible verses written especially for her, like "Wives, . . . submit to your husbands as to the Lord." We knew what the Bible said. Trying to live these words out in the center of the storm, with nerves exposed and raw, we fell into sin—not sin that involved other people; we simply weren't walking in love. We grew distant and irritable with each other.

We were troubled by how little time we were able to devote to our other three children—they needed us too. How could we ever create a "normal" home environment for them? It seemed such an irony to have worked so hard to have a nice family home on a lovely property but to so seldom be there as a family.

We were spending an inordinate amount of time at the hospital, devoting the bulk of our energy to Alex. Our middle children were four and two, unique stages that require special attention. Then, of course, there was Ryan, who had joined us just two days before the accident. New babies aren't exactly low maintenance. The first weeks are critical in forming the child's cognitive skills, personality, and normal development in bonding with the parents, especially the mother. We didn't want Ryan to be neglected in any way.

+++ I have to be honest and say that Kevin and Beth greatly struggled in their marriage. Many times I came to the house to speak with them, counsel them, and pray with them. Those were dark days.

One time I was so troubled in my spirit, feeling the weight of spiritual oppression over that marriage, that I called one of the men in our fellowship, and the two of us went over to the Malarkey house to pray. I didn't knock on the door. We just began praying, walking around their house seven times, praying all the time. It is an absolute miracle, an absolute proof there is a God in Heaven, that their marriage survived and that they are together today. Without God, there is no possible way their marriage would have survived.

Pastor Gary Brown,
the Malarkeys' pastor at the time of the accident +++

It just felt like too much to carry. Beth and I, needless to say, had some long talks with our Creator: *Lord, You know this is far more than we can handle, on any number of fronts. We need You as we never have before. We've prayed without ceasing for Alex, as have countless other people. But we must lay before You so many other requests as well. We have three other children who covet our attention. We have bills we cannot pay. We have our marriage, and the two of us each need personal strength and daily energy to keep going. We can only ask for Your wisdom, Lord, and claim Your promise that You will never desert us.*

Our House Takes a Battering

Our tag-team parenting lifestyle continued into the cold weeks of winter. One of us would "jump into the ring" with the three children at home, while the other would stand watch at the hospital. Then we'd switch places.

One evening, I was home with the kids. Little by little, icy rain descended over the entire area of Bellefontaine, but we were warm inside. *Let the ice fall*, I thought. Then, with a flicker, the lights went out and the house was enveloped in darkness. We had lost all electricity. Packing a bag quickly before the worst of the ice storm hit, I had to find somewhere for the kids and me to spend the night, which, other than driving in a developing ice storm, didn't prove to be too difficult. Once we'd settled into our temporary digs at Beth's sister's home and I'd put the kids down for the night, I realized we weren't too much the worse for wear.

The next morning, I returned to our house to see how things were. Was the power back on? The house isn't visible from the road, and no sooner had I pulled into the two-hundred-foot-long driveway than I had to stop the car. A tree had fallen across the front of the driveway, preventing me from driving farther. *No problem*, I thought. *I'll walk.*

I jumped over the downed tree and carefully made my way up the slippery driveway, looking from side to side at the destruction the ice storm had brought. Trees were down everywhere, enveloped in thick sheets of ice. With one across the road, how many would be down on the rest of the property? I dialed my father to tell him what I was finding. "Hey, Dad, you won't believe this. There are trees down all over my property. This is unbelievable. Well, at least one didn't fall on our—" Timing is everything. Just as I said that, I rounded the bend to see that a huge tree had fallen directly across the center of our roof.

"Uh, Dad, looks like I'll have to call you back."

I stared with incredulity, taking in the scene. If the tree falling on our house had been the only thing we had to deal with, it might have seemed more significant in my mind. Given that Alex's life was hanging in the balance, it just didn't register as that big of a deal. Sure, I had mixed emotions, but when your child is only barely clinging to life, everything else falls into perspective.

I called Pastor Brown. I knew he would come after getting the word out to others. And he brought a chainsaw and hard hats! We put the hard hats on and entered the house. There was still no power, and even though it was mid-afternoon, all was dark inside. Without knowing what kind of structural damage there was, we moved along carefully.

It could have been better; it could have been worse. The roof would have to be replaced, but it had kept the tree from breaking through to the floor of the house. And of course, there was plenty of damage to our possessions. Many repairs would be necessary—just what we needed. I thought of our beleaguered family and sighed: when it rains, it pours.

Beth, the three younger children, and I slept in the basement of Beth's sister's home for a week. We were very grateful that Kris was willing to take us in. By now, we were accustomed to sleeping in all kinds of places. For baby Ryan, this was simply the norm; he had spent only one night under his family's own roof. We were all becoming a little tougher in the boot camp that our life had become.

Ten men cut up and removed all the fallen trees and the bits of trunk and branches that had come down on our property. And once again, an army of earthly angels seemed to descend upon us in the middle of our trial. It was another lesson in learning to trust the goodness and providence of God.

The repair work would be undertaken in fits and starts for more than two years. Half the roof needed to be pulled out and rebuilt. The deck, interior walls, and ceiling all needed to be replaced as well. I hired a man from our church to oversee the project. He and his crew went to work. Over time, it became clear that the roofing crew, about fifteen people in all, were using their vacation time and

---

+++ When Kevin called back and told me about the tree on the house, my first response was to laugh—not a laugh of callousness, but a laugh of joy at the goodness of God. I truly mean that. For me, the question isn't, "Why do bad things happen to good people?" but "Why does anything good happen at all?" We certainly don't deserve it.

I told Kevin, "First, consider that the power went out. What a great blessing. Had it not gone out, Kevin, you would have been in the house with the kids when the tree struck the roof. Second, you badly needed to replace your roof anyway. Now you'll get a brand-new one, and your insurance is going to pay for it! And third, I have a question, Kevin: Which trees were taken down in this storm? All the weak ones! The strong trees are still standing. You've received a natural pruning, making your property safer and healthier, leaving the strong trees for your family to enjoy. By next July, you won't be able to tell a single tree was taken down."

The hand of God was everywhere to be seen in this situation, but, as I pointed out to Kevin, we have to be willing to see it—to receive it as God's good in our lives.

Dr. William Malarkey, Kevin's father +++

---

taking days off from their jobs to work on someone else's problems in the dead of winter. These people were true servants and somehow managed to convey the perspective that *I* was serving *them* by allowing them to come and fix my house. They worked as if they hadn't enjoyed such an amazing privilege in a long time.

It's ingrained in us to earn our own way, to pay back any little favor, and never to be on the debt side of the ledger. Not long after I "hired" the foreman, I pulled him aside and assured him that I would be paying all the workers. Just as I was emphasizing my point, one of the men overheard our conversation.

"Don't you get it, Kevin? This is the best-paying job I've ever had."

"Owe nothing to anyone—except for your obligation to love one another" (Romans 13:8). The chill and damage of winter's worst ice storm was no match for the warmth we found in those beautiful examples of Christ's love.

Our Bank Account Takes a Battering

We had already been in a tight spot financially before any of this happened. Now it was nearly impossible to avoid thinking of our lack of money.

On the very morning of the accident, I had sat in church and reflected on the financial challenges our family must confront, since Ryan's birth had not been covered by our health-care plan. Now we had Alex's situation, and I didn't know where the money was going to come from to cover his astronomical hospital expenses—this, of course, during a time when it was virtually impossible for me to give my energy, time, and focus to my counseling practice. I felt pulled in so many directions, and I know Beth did too.

One afternoon, as I sat in Alex's room pondering all of this, a hospital representative came in.

"Mr. Malarkey, may I talk with you?" she asked.

"Of course. May I ask what about?"

"Yes. Well, we need to discuss the payment of your account."

I stiffened but maintained my composure. This was strangely reminiscent of the time I was given the bill for my wedding reception while the event was still in progress. I walked into the hallway with the woman and said, "Now, what seems to be the problem?"

She said, "I really was wondering if you could fill out some paperwork."

"Well," I said, "I have a special situation. I've recently switched to a medical expense sharing group, and to be frank, I'm not exactly sure where things stand."

I was embarrassed. We had used hundreds of thousands of dollars' worth of hospital time, facilities, and surgical practice. Unbeknownst to me, it would be millions before long, and I wasn't clear on where the money was going to come from.

"I understand," she said. "But don't you want to check into Medicaid?"

"I don't know much about how those things work, but isn't it for, you know, people who are truly poor? I can't imagine that we would qualify."

"People often think that," she explained. "They're often surprised by how it works out—particularly when they have a large number of children. Don't you have four? Each child raises the income limit."

"I had no idea."

It didn't take long for me to crunch the numbers, and it turned out that, given my current income and the arrival of Ryan in November, we fit just under the limit for Medicaid. What a weight suddenly flew off my shoulders! Medicaid would pay every penny of Alex's bill, and the coverage would be retroactive to November 1, 2004, for the entire family. We owed more than $10,000 for Ryan's birth, and just like that it would be taken care of.

I had already received two bills that totaled $200,000. The aggregate total of medical costs ended up well into seven figures. What I owed out of pocket to Children's Hospital was a grand total of $14, which, it turned out, was an accounting error. I didn't even owe that much!

How can I describe my feelings? Overwhelmed. Grateful. Humble. Ashamed.

Yes, Lord, You've made Your point—again, I prayed. *I carry all this burden of worry, and You cover everything in Your plans. I haven't understood that my income struggles and my drop in salary were part of Your perfect plan! The amount of my loss is far exceeded by the bills that I don't have to face—and even if I'd still used traditional insurance, it would have combined with Medicaid and still left me with a massive bill that could take many years to pay. But You knew in advance how to bless us. Why can't I ever learn to walk in faith, to trust Your will?*

Out of the Prison of Self-Pity

My dad, as usual, put it best: "If you weren't broke, you'd be bankrupt."

He had a point. As a matter of fact, I never knew him not to have one. My father has the wisest advice of anyone who has ever counseled me.

During the early part of our experience with Alex and the accident, Dad offered me his perspective once again, and it served me well. When the accident occurred, he was speaking at a medical conference in Europe. He quickly flew home to Ohio. As soon as he spotted me at the hospital, he put his arm around me and said, "Son, many people in the world would love for this to be their worst problem."

+++

Does our daily focus on the ordinary events of life dampen our awareness of the providential and miraculous events occurring in and around us all the time?

Dr. William Malarkey,
Kevin's father

I realize many people just don't get that point of view, and some would say that he was being insensitive with this comment. But I knew my dad. His incredible perspective on life and what is really important gives him amazing power in everyday living. How many times did I come to him with a problem when I was growing up? And how many times did he patiently listen and offer good advice? But I knew every single time what I was going to hear before I left the room—he would always bring up someone we both knew who was struggling in life to help me better comprehend the scope of my own problem.

I came to understand the wisdom of this approach. Self-pity imprisons us in the walls of our own self-absorption. The whole world shrinks down to the size of our problem, and the more we dwell on it, the smaller we are and the larger the problem seems to grow. Awareness of others is a healthy antidote to this self-focus.

We're not the only ones with issues, and usually our own struggles are far from the worst we know about. There is never a moment in life when it's impossible to have a heart filled with gratitude—no matter what happens. A catastrophic event, such as our accident, puts that philosophy to the test. But even then it's true, and Dad dared to apply it as his grandson lay in the valley of the shadow of death.

I didn't need to know just how unfortunate I was. I needed to be reminded of the truth: my struggles were far from the only ones out there, and I still had much to be grateful for. I can't imagine any outlook on life that is wiser or more grounded. I recall sitting in the waiting room of the ICU, watching news of the tsunami that hit Indonesia at the end of the year. Nearly 230,000 people in about a dozen countries were killed; 43,000 of them simply vanished without a trace.

I sat in my chair at the hospital and watched the TV screen as a home floated along the coast. I thought to myself, *I still have Alex, who is alive by the grace of God. I still have my home.* Okay, that home needed some major repairs, but I still had it. And even when my house crunched under the force of the tree trunk, I could still say, "Many people all over the world would love for this to be their worst day."

+++

I remember telling my father that I'd been happy each of the first sixty days of Alex's coma—and I'd cried on fifty-seven of them.

Kevin Malarkey

My dad doesn't believe in the existence of a bad day. I find that holding this philosophy makes a great difference in our state of contentment. The tougher life became, the more good we saw in people and in God.

It's possible to know peace and pain at the same time, believe it or not. Life can be rough yet still feel right. Even as I wept at times, I knew my family was aligned with the will of God. I could say, with the old hymn, *It is well with my soul.*

Even so, in moments of reflection, I've asked myself, *Do you wish the accident had never happened?* That's an easy call. Yes—and no. From a strictly human or physical perspective, of course I wish that the accident had never happened! But I am not merely a mass of molecules, incoherently careening through time and space. I am a child of God, destined for another world, a world before which this one pales in significance. Our spiritual preparation for the *next* world is to be the priority of *this* life. As the accident has brought Alex and me—and untold thousands—a deeper life with God, then my answer to this question has to be different. I have chosen to view the accident as integral to my life.

What if we could go back and rewrite the scripts for our lives? With what I know now, I could avoid a lot of pain by bypassing the future laid out for me. But I would also be sidestepping the countless blessings of God, present and future. I could never have peace about that.

It's not a matter of God's planning for my son to suffer, but of God's planning to use all of this to do wonderful things that bless many lives—my son and the rest of my family included. Nothing good ever comes to pass without a price. It's a very difficult thing to understand, but ask yourself, what if Jesus—who *did* have foreknowledge of His crucifixion—had turned and walked away?

I hate pain and suffering, especially when it affects those I love more than anything else in this world. But I trust God; I trust Him implicitly to turn sadness into joy and mourning into dancing. I can't wait to watch Alex dance!

Can Alex Hear Us?

Beth and I were with Alex every day, but we knew his siblings would eventually need to see him too. Determining the right timing was a tough judgment call. It would be hard for them to understand why Alex would not be able to talk to them or play with them, and he was in a strange room with lots of scary machinery.

A few weeks into Alex's coma, we decided to bring Aaron to see his brother. At four, he was the sibling closest to Alex in both age and friendship. Alex had a few friends, but his best buddy was always Aaron. They were inseparable. In fact, from ages four to six we have almost no pictures of Alex without Aaron. Doesn't that say it all? They played sports together, they played with action figures together, they ran around outside together, they climbed trees together, and, yes, they disobeyed their parents together!

We spent time talking with Aaron, preparing him for the experience. In our "parental wisdom," we told him Alex was sleeping. While we spoke to Alex all the time, hoping that on some level he could hear and understand, we didn't want Aaron to have unrealistic expectations.

Aaron was keen on bringing Alex a gift: a G.I. Joe action figure. We told him we thought that was a fine idea. Beth and I had a friend, "Mr. Jeff," who was also close to our children. He accompanied Aaron and me, carrying Aaron in his arms, and the three of us entered Alex's room.

My radar was on high alert, keeping a close eye on Aaron. How would he handle this strange setting for his beloved big brother? In the wonderful way of a child, he took it all in stride and was delighted to see Alex. It's so easy to underestimate what children can handle.

We held Aaron above the reclining body of his brother, and he began showing Alex the cool toy he'd brought him. In better times, the two of them had loved playing together with action figures. In many ways, Alex had been the ideal big brother for a little boy.

I wondered just how difficult it was for Aaron on the inside, how much he was missing his favorite playmate.

"See how G.I. Joe can move his legs? He's running!" said Aaron, manipulating the limbs on the action figure and making all the appropriate sound effects. "See, he has the kung-fu grip!"

He demonstrated all the features of the toy just as if the two of them were alone, having a great time as they always had.

I should have been satisfied with Aaron's relaxed, happy demeanor, but I couldn't keep myself from worrying that at some point, Aaron's little heart might be hurt because big brother Alex remained unresponsive. In as gentle and nurturing a way as I could, I said, "Remember, Aaron, your brother is asleep. He can't hear you."

Aaron turned around, looking me straight in the eye, and announced with absolute confidence, "He can hear me."

He was only four, but he spoke with all the assurance of one who had all the facts. He turned back around as if to say, *What is it about these things that adults just don't get?* and continued demonstrating the action figure's features to comatose Alex.

I might as well have told him the sky was green. "What are you talking about, the sky is green? Anyone can see the sky is blue. Of course Alex can hear me."

Jeff and I simply looked at each other and shrugged our shoulders. Can a child see and understand certain things that skeptical adult minds can't?

Miracles at Christmas

The world never slows down to accommodate a family crisis. Our lives remained an absolute blur of appointments, discussions, and medications, even as a myriad of people cared for our other children and many of our own needs. The one constant around which everything swirled was Alex in his long sleep. It had been a month since our full family of six had occupied one room at the same time.

Even as Alex was inches away in body but worlds away in spirit, we began to prepare him for his own return to life. We remained confident it would happen, so we believed we had to prepare. Very gently, we'd lift him from his bed and place him in a wheelchair for short periods of time, a painstaking, methodical process. First we would move him to the edge of the bed so that his legs dangled over the side. Beth would slide behind him, both to support him and to give him big hugs. What was at first a series of carefully executed moves became another routine in our lives.

One day, something changed. As Beth went through the process, Alex's lips formed into a slight but unmistakable smile. We looked at each other to confirm that we hadn't imagined it. Our son was smiling. We looked at each other in amazement as tears of joy began to flow. God was so good to give us this little encouraging sign. Maybe Aaron was right: *What do you mean he can't hear us?* But it turned out to be only a momentary flash, and Alex was off again to somewhere we couldn't go.

At Christmas, we paused to consider that it had been six weeks since the accident. In some ways, it seemed like six years. For the first time, the hospital allowed us to bring all the children into Alex's room. For the third day ever, all six of us were in one place. We were able to open a few presents together and to take a family Christmas picture.

It's another idea that is difficult to explain unless you've walked in our shoes, but this was one of my best Christmases ever. By now, we had learned to take nothing for granted. Our son was in a coma, our new home was in shambles, and the presence of God was more real to us than ever before. Just being together was itself a special gift from God. We held each other close and prayed that the Lord would bring us even closer—to one another and to Him—in 2005.

+++ Several months after Alex's accident, I was at a run review. This is when a physician reviews patient charts with the flight crew to assess the quality of care given and educate us on a patient's particular injury or illness. During a review, no information is given that could be used to identify a person. When the doctor got to one patient, however, the details sounded familiar.

We were told the flight crew had done a good job. Then we were shown an X-ray revealing that the patient's skull was separated from the spinal column. The doctor concluded that the patient had expired because this injury was simply incompatible with life.

I wasn't 100 percent sure this was Alex's case because no identifying information had been given. I later discovered, however, that this was indeed Alex. Normally, the physician would have been correct to say a patient in this condition had died; however, the Lord was taking care of Alex, and Alex was not dead.

Dave Knopp, paramedic +++

In the midst of all the joy of being together, my eyes moved from one child to another, then to Beth, but my mind wandered into the future of mounting bills. If it seems that my thoughts seesawed between keeping my mind on Jesus, the amazing financial provision

God had made, and the mountain of trials we were climbing—that's exactly how it was. At one point, I triumphed in faith; at another time, I allowed the angry waves to obscure the Redeemer. I used to read the stories of the Israelites and wonder, *How could those ungrateful people have been so quick to take their eyes off God after all the miraculous things He did for them?* I didn't have to wonder anymore. I was just like them.

Yet, in the midst of all these temporal concerns, we were about to see the world we were living in collide with the world Alex was experiencing.

From Alex

Angels

An angel of the Lord appeared among them, and the radiance of the Lord's glory surrounded them. They were terrified, but the angel reassured them. "Don't be afraid!"

LUKE 2:9-10

Angels aren't boys or girls. They are neither.

They are completely white and have wings.

Some are not as big as Daddy thought they would be— only about two feet tall. Other angels, especially the ones in Heaven, are larger. The angels have visited me many times, and I have felt afraid when more than one comes. Later on, when my daddy and I were able to talk about these things, he told me that maybe these angels are small in size to help me with my fear—I don't know.

They have different jobs. One just makes me feel better—I get more courage. Another helps me open my mouth and make words. One had his hands on my chest—to help me become stronger, to help me breathe. I always see the angels when they come, and even when I couldn't talk, they could hear me. At the same time they do their jobs, they make beautiful songs for God.

One time when the angels were with me in my hospital room, my daddy asked me if I wanted to sing with them. I said yes, so we played a worship song—I couldn't sing with my mouth, but I was singing with the angels—they could hear me. This was in the days when I had to talk to people with special signals—but I didn't need to talk that way to the angels!

People have told me that after I am with the angels my face is glowing—like a thousand Christmas mornings. It's funny that I could usually only smile with just one corner of my mouth, but that my smiles after the angels' visits were huge. I've heard about Stephen's face in the Bible when he looked up to Heaven. Maybe my face looks like that?

There are different kinds of angels. People often want me to describe them, but this is hard! I can only use words like *magnificent*, *awesome*, and *incredible*.

The angels talk to me about themselves and about me. Some of the angels are messengers, and some are warriors, and some are worshipers. One group of angels guards the walls of Heaven. These are the toughest angels of all. They are at all the posts on the wall, and the main post is the heavenly gates.

My daddy asked if it was like the Great Wall of China. No, it isn't—how can I describe this? But the angels are spread out like that.

There are lots of buildings in Heaven, but I only really notice the Temple. God never leaves the throne in the Temple. There is a scroll in a glass container. It describes the end times. No one can read this scroll but Jesus.

So there are a lot of different angels. The one thing they all have in common is that they are awesome!

They also make me feel calm.

CHAPTER 6

WE MEET ANOTHER WORLD

As men and women devoted to science,
they had no explanation for how this could
have occurred inside their hospital.

As DECEMBER APPROACHED, so many incredible things had happened since the accident that we sensed that, other than Alex's complete recovery, the biggest events were behind us. There had already been more than enough cause for praise. After all, Alex was alive, and we felt that we were being held firmly in the loving hands of God. We had experienced love and spiritual support, not to mention material support, in a manner we had not thought possible. God's fountain of supply seemed never ending.

Hillbilly had said he sensed the Spirit of God moving in a powerful way. We were soon to be plunged deeply into a world I had known only superficially.

Science Is Confounded

Alex's first surgery came during the month of the accident. A hole needed to be cut in his throat—a stoma—so that a ventilator could be attached and the tubes could be removed from his throat. This operation is called a tracheotomy. The surgeons would also make a small hole for a stomach tube, through which he could receive fluids and medication, as he had no ability to swallow.

How I longed to see Alex without all those monitors, machines, tubes, and wires! When the medical staff began unhooking him for the surgery, however, I became increasingly anxious. Alex needed all that stuff to survive. Could I trust that they really knew what they were doing? Silly question, I know, but in the moment, all of this was quite unnerving. As a parent looking on with absolutely no power to protect, to expedite the situation, or to keep my child safe, the feeling of helplessness was unavoidable.

Even so, from the first day of the crisis, we took every opportunity to hug Alex, speak comforting words to him, and generally treat him as if he fully understood everything. We decided from the beginning to treat him the same as our other children. We spoke to Alex as if his eyes were open and he were listening, nodding, and smiling—just not offering replies. We encouraged him. We told him that God was with him. Our words were truer and more wonderful than we could possibly have guessed.

The surgery went well, according to the doctors who filled us in later. Alex now had two new holes in his body. The medical experts had never thought he would make it far enough to have these procedures. We believed the surgery was simply one more positive step in getting our son back.

As Alex's condition stabilized a bit, the doctors began exploring next steps. They had told us early on that they eventually planned to fuse the vertebrae in Alex's neck. Without surgical intervention, they said, his neck would never be stable.

By the end of November, they were considering an interim step: attaching a "halo" brace to Alex's head that would hold his neck in place. They scheduled an MRI of Alex's neck for November 30; later that same day, they told us, they might attach the halo. This brace, a metal ring that secures to the skull with pins, would keep his head and neck immobile and could aid in healing the area of greatest injury.

For the doctors, these options were exciting possibilities. For Beth and me they both seemed like steps in the wrong direction. We were holding out for the big victory. We were praying for full healing.

The doctors continued their deliberations, unaware of our struggles. After examining the results of Alex's MRI, they decided to scrap the halo plan. Yet they continued to consider the vertebrae fusion.

The downside to the surgery was that Alex would never regain full movement in his neck—and what would that mean when he was fully healed? This issue didn't concern the medical staff. We weren't really certain what to do, so we talked it over, prayed, and decided to give the surgeons the green light. A date was set, and the army of prayer warriors again assumed their fighting stance—on their knees.

And then we received stunning news. By the end of December, the doctors concluded the vertebrae had healed well without intervention, or rather without *medical* intervention. "We're not sure what happened," the neurosurgeon told me, "but we don't need to do the surgery."

I was ecstatic! "That's okay, Doctor," I told him. "We understand; in fact, we know what happened. There is a Physician who has been healing people since the beginning of time, and Alex is one of His patients."

The word went out to Alex's Army. They rejoiced. But they were not surprised.

We were confident that God had intervened in time and space, responding to the prayers of the saints. Sometime later we discovered other intriguing events that occurred around the same time.

Not long after the surgery was scheduled and then canceled, we heard from Sue, who wanted to tell us about her own experience with Alex. The story she related constituted another miracle in our remarkable experience—and preceded still another miracle.

Visitors in the Night

We'd seen people doing the work of angels—calling 911, climbing into the car to pray with Alex, riding in the helicopter, even showing up to serve God by working on our home. But Sue's report indicated we were moving into a new arena—one I had no direct experience with.

Sue had responded to an early appeal for prayer warriors who would be willing to stay with Alex overnight. On one such evening, she quietly entered Alex's room and settled in a chair opposite his bed. She spent the next few hours reading to Alex and praying for him. At around 3 a.m., as her head was bowed in prayer, she heard the sounds of water flowing from the faucet in Alex's room. That seemed a little odd to her, but since there were no doors in the ICU units, she assumed that one of the nurses had come in to Alex's room and was washing her hands. Finally, she couldn't help herself and looked up, only to see that no one was there.

She bowed her head again, and after a few moments the sound of flowing water filled Alex's room for a second time. She looked up—nothing. She went back to prayer. And for the third time she heard water flowing. When she looked up, she saw nothing. Though she thought it was strange, she was there for a specific purpose, so she resumed praying.

Then she was suddenly filled with the knowledge, in her spirit, that there were three angels present in the room, standing behind Alex, with their hands on his neck. She wasn't looking—she saw nothing with her eyes—but she *knew* and *felt* their presence.

Before leaving, one of the angels told her, "There is more to do, but this is all for now." Sue told us she was convinced that angels were ministering to and looking after Alex—especially in the middle of the night.

Beth read and reread Sue's e-mail. We were both caught up in a sense of wonder that angels had visited our son and that our friend, who hadn't seen them, was as confident they were there as if she had. It's easy to discount this sort of thing, but there was more information for us to consider. Upon pondering that e-mail, Beth wondered about the timing of the events Sue reported. She pulled out the prayer/visiting schedule and began poring over the dates for people staying overnight with Alex. The information was easily available because every detail of this prayer ministry was highly organized.

When Beth found that night's record, she called me over. "Look at this, Kevin. The record is right here. Sue was praying over Alex the evening before doctors planned on putting the halo on Alex. The angels were there the evening before that procedure was . . .

canceled." Beth looked into my eyes with a quiet, confident expression as if to say, "It's happening."

A surge of hope coursed through me. *Oh, God, help my unbelief. You are the God of miracles.*

A few days later the phone rang.

"Hello," answered Beth.

"Hello, my name is Melissa. I'm so sorry to bother you, but I had to call you. It's about Alex. I've been praying for him."

"It's no bother at all. We greatly appreciate everyone who is lifting him up in prayer."

"Well, I don't want to take you off guard, but something has happened, and I wanted to tell you about it. Is this a good time?"

"Sure. What's on your mind?"

"I've had a vision . . . from God . . . about Alex and angels. I'm an artist, and I had to paint the vision. May I send it to you? I'd like you to have it."

"Sure, we'd love to see it."

After Sue's experience, the idea of visions from God was less jarring than it would have been prior to this entire ordeal. We were eager to see what this woman had painted—what she was sure God had shown her.

When the package containing the painting arrived, we carefully unwrapped it. After the last piece of tissue paper was gingerly removed, we stared, awestruck at the image. Clearly depicted were three angels standing behind Alex's bed with their hands on his neck. For the longest time, we just sat and stared, drinking in the amazing encouragement of our awesome God. God truly had sent angels to minister to Alex.

We soon got on the phone with Sue. She had never met nor

spoken with the artist. Beth described the painting in detail. Sue, too, was amazed as she confirmed that the painting captured exactly what God had revealed to her during her prayer watch. We were reminded of Jesus' words in Matthew 18:10 about little children: "For I tell you that in heaven their angels are always in the presence of my heavenly Father."

We scanned the picture and posted it on PrayforAlex.com so that everyone could be blessed by it. More than ever, it was clear that God was involved in our situation in a remarkable way and that the result of it was that the Lord would be glorified. Our hope for the future continued to build.

We give thanks to God for Alex's angels.

Awakening

As the holiday season ended and a new year began, Alex's long sleep continued. His body was still with us; his spirit, unaccounted for. We held on in faith that God would bring him back to us, but there was another looming issue. The hospital medical staff was deliberating about where they would send Alex. They wanted to discharge him, but where? The conversation took on an awkward tone. Everyone other than the ICU staff seemed afraid of the ventilator and the issues surrounding it.

Finally, the doctors began talking about sending Alex to the rehabilitation unit. Beth and I couldn't make sense of that idea—how do you rehabilitate a child in a coma? We soon discovered the answer: you don't. You "rehab" the parents. This was going to be all about training us, so that we could eventually take Alex home.

We began to learn how to feed Alex, give him medication, clean him, and monitor the equipment and everything else necessary to

+++ Here is a letter I wrote to Alex on January 6, 2005:

Alex,

I've prayed for you so often, and for so many things.

I asked God for His healing hands, and I touched your entire body.

I asked God to make every cell in your body totally healthy.

I prayed for the hurts in your brain stem and spinal cord to get better; I prayed for you to regain lost functions.

I asked God to allow you to *come forth*, as Lazarus did. I urged Him to restore in you the awareness necessary to become a rehab patient, rather than a neurosurgery patient on the rehab unit.

They don't think you can do it, Alex. I guess they don't know our God as well as we do; perhaps they haven't seen what He will do when we trust His promises. The doctors speak of ventilators, but I asked God that the day would never come when a ventilator would enter our house; it wouldn't be necessary, because you'd be breathing freely and independently when you came home.

Alex, I'm praying harder than I ever have. I'm believing bold possibilities that, in the past, I might never have dared to believe.

I prayed Ephesians 3:20 for you:

Now all glory to God, who is able, through his mighty power
at work within us, to accomplish infinitely more than we might
ask or think.

I saw you in the words of Psalm 91:1-5:

Those who live in the shelter of the Most High
will find rest in the shadow of the Almighty.

This I declare about the LORD:
He alone is my refuge, my place of safety;
*   he is my God, and I trust him.*
For he will rescue you from every trap
*   and protect you from deadly disease.*
He will cover you with his feathers.
*   He will shelter you with his wings.*
*   His faithful promises are your armor and protection.*
Do not be afraid of the terrors of the night.

Alex, I will not be dishonest and claim I've had no sad moments. I'm missing terribly the fun we had together. But I feel so very blessed to be your daddy here on earth. You exceed every expectation I'd ever had for a son.

I pray for Satan's defeat every day. I pray that God Himself breathes new life into you, and when I see you, I bend down and try to breathe my breath into your nostrils and mouth. I see how you don't like me doing that!

My son, I promise to love you and to care for you, no matter what the future holds, as long as you and I are both alive. I am in you and you are in me; that will never change.

I pray that God will align my will with His, and I will praise Him for whatever He may do. I praise Him and worship Him each day as we watch the miracle named Alexander.

I love you more today than yesterday.

Daddy

Kevin Malarkey ✦✦✦

get our son through each day. The "final exam" was for each of us to handle all of Alex's care for a twenty-four-hour period, including pulling an all-nighter. Someone mishandled the paperwork, so I actually got to do that drill twice. I didn't mind.

Alex finally left the ICU for a new room in the rehab unit. The plan, as we learned in our first meeting, was to keep him there for about one month. After all, he wasn't a true rehab patient, so he couldn't benefit from the services there. Beth and I had a month to become skilled at caring for all of Alex's needs, after which he would be discharged from the hospital.

But I had different plans.

I looked around and saw all the exercise equipment and the trained therapists. I could visualize Alex benefiting from the whole environment. As I told our followers on PrayforAlex.com, I wanted Alex to wake up and take advantage of all that was there for him in rehab. He wouldn't need to be fully conscious, just sufficiently aware to meet the threshold requirements of response.

This was a true crisis moment. The doctors had no further expectations for Alex's recovery, but we did—and we wanted to keep him in that place that would most help him on the long road to recovery. The hospital had done its duty, we had done all that we could do, and now it was time for Alex to show up. It was up to Alex—which meant, of course, that it was up to God.

I prayed, *Lord, wake Alex up! Touch his brain stem today and send him back to us, because this is his chance to begin getting better. This is the place to get the tools he needs.*

I really believed, too. I felt in my spirit that a change was coming very soon. Already Alex was beginning ever so slightly to track activity in the room with his eyes. His condition was stable, and his meds were manageable. He seemed to be sleeping better in the rehab unit, and we believed he was on the verge of being ready to "power heal."

Beth and I tried to keep seeing the forest and not just the trees. That is, we knew that the big picture was all about God's doing something that couldn't be explained by human means. We were ready to care for our boy in a permanent coma if it came to that, but we didn't believe this was how the story would end. So we asked all our friends and the outstanding Alex's Army to join us in petitioning the Lord. We pleaded with Him to intervene once more in our son's medical condition. Our long-term goal was to have Alex at home with us, where he belonged. A date was set, and we called on our army of prayer warriors once again.

There was a certain amount of skepticism floating around concerning this strategy. Some felt that caring for him at home would never work. One nurse, for example, told us, "I can take care of him in a hospital like this one, but I don't think I could handle it in a house." She and others believed that a nursing home was the answer. Nursing homes are viable solutions for others—but we wanted our son to be in his own bed, under our roof. We couldn't imagine any other outcome.

We knew things would be difficult, and we believed we were ready for that reality.

Breakthrough

One morning the phone rang, and that cheerful voice I knew so well greeted me.

"Kevin!" It was my dad.

"Hey, Dad, what's up?"

"Kevin, he's on his way back! He's on his way back!"

"What do you mean?"

"I went to see Alex this morning, and he followed my wedding ring with his eyes—he was *tracking*!"

My heart beat wildly, and I wasted no time in getting to the hospital. It wasn't the first time I'd heard hopeful observations about Alex—people tended to see, or think they saw, facial expressions. Some were certain he had moved a hand or a toe. There are times when we're so eager, we see what we want to see.

But these words were coming from my dad, Dr. William Malarkey, distinguished physician. He knew what to look for, and he didn't deal in manufactured hope. He had never once made such a declaration. His excitement got me excited.

I still think of January 8 as the day my son emerged from his coma, but it wasn't that cut-and-dried. He didn't wake up suddenly, as if from a nap. He'd been gone for nearly two months. He had disappeared from us in an instant, but his return to the Alex we knew would take much longer, given the damage to his spine and his head. The doctors were very skeptical about any future abilities he might have, or even his ability to think. But from this day onward, our Alex began his long journey home. It was as if the light of his mind was being turned on with a slow dimmer switch. Every day brought Alex another step back into our world.

I was ready to celebrate when the hospital agreed to admit Alex to rehab. My prayer had been answered, and it didn't matter how unlikely it might have seemed to others—God had come through. Now Alex could begin to work with the rehab assistants, and that would make all the difference. I felt that I knew how much strength and determination was inside Alex, and again I was certain that rehab was going to be a smashing success. The rehab doctors were now in charge, but we considered the Great Physician to be the one with the ultimate prognosis.

Alex's Army rejoiced with us as we shared all these new developments with our community at PrayforAlex.com. And the Army kept praying.

Slaphappy

Even with the thrilling signs that Alex was coming back, he was still in a thick fog. Some days it seemed he was charging ahead; other days made us feel we had lost ground. We tried absolutely everything we could think of to shine our light through that fog and guide him home. Everyone who came into the room had his or her own little act to spark Alex's awareness. People told jokes, made funny faces, made body noises (real and simulated), and even lightly tickled a body that we were assured had no feeling.

Where are you, Alex? We prayed, we spoke positively, and we truly believed . . . most of the time. When my moments of doubt emerged, I carefully hid them. No one could really measure the impact of the severe damage to his brain and spinal cord. Mental, physical, and emotional functioning might be intact—medically speaking—or it might be destroyed forever. We simply couldn't know.

When I thought about that, fear gripped me. It wasn't about paralysis or his breathing on a ventilator. I could handle any of that. What terrified me was the idea of never getting my son back. I had moments when I would have paid any conceivable price just to talk to my Alex. So I kept up my one-sided conversations, just as if we were having the talks we'd always had. Everyone else made funny faces, performed silly dances, and tried any wild strategy to pull him out of the mist. At this point, nothing looked unusual in that room—people had tried everything but standing on their heads.

Maybe brothers close in age are the ones who know best how to make each other laugh. It was Aaron who finally made it happen.

Aaron came up with his own idea about how to spark Alex's attention. Aaron put his face near Alex's and then gave his own face a hard *smack!* Aaron then repeatedly smacked his own face. Something about Aaron's monkey business got through, and after a few more slaps, a genuine smile broke out across Alex's face. I'd never seen anything so beautiful, even if it took Aaron slapping himself to bring it on. Aaron kept slapping his cheeks, and Alex's smile kept growing. This was no muscular reflex—it was a *grin*. Everyone present could see it, and the whole room let out a spontaneous victory cheer. Aaron was very pleased with his success and redoubled his efforts, slapping himself even more vigorously. I then stepped in and prevented Aaron from doing further damage to his handsome face. He'd done a great job, and it was time to give his facial tissue a break!

From this point onward, Alex never completely vanished back into the fog. He had an awareness of the room and the people in it, and he clearly knew when we were talking to him.

I wrote a poem at the time to express the power of God we felt was at work in Alex:

Alex cannot walk
Jesus walked on water

Alex cannot talk
God spoke the universe into existence

Alex cannot breathe
The Holy Spirit is the breath of life

Therefore . . .

I will not look to the world
But to the WORD

I will not look to my son
But to my FATHER

I will not see with my eyes
But with my HEART

I will not fall victim
To the prison of circumstance

I will worship my God
And abide in his hope

Let it be . . .

Going to Work

Now the rehab therapists had something to work with, and they began interacting with Alex in various ways.

"Alex," the speech therapist asked, "can you tell me how old you are?"

We all watched with great anticipation, but I had an extra level of intensity waiting for his reply. By this point, my one obsession was to ask Alex to forgive me for what I had done. The moment I desired more than any other was within reach. But then smiles began to fade as we looked from Alex to the therapist. Alex only stared ahead.

"Alex," continued the therapist, "do you know how old you are? What is your age?"

Alex didn't respond. The more the therapist questioned him, the more a confused expression etched its way across his brow. My eyes darted between Alex and the therapist. What could all this mean? Discreetly we were summoned out of the room, and the therapist offered her thoughts.

"We want to be careful about broad pronouncements in cases like these, but we also want to be realistic about where we are. The reality of this situation may be not only that Alex didn't respond—that he didn't know the answer to the question—but that he *can't* respond."

Can't respond? my mind screamed in fear. *No!* Up to this point, there was never a doubt in my mind that Alex would come back and be our Alex. I had never anticipated the idea, even for a moment, that Alex might have severe brain damage. Of course Alex would come back and we could have that one conversation I had agonized over a thousand times—the one question I so desperately longed to ask: "Alex, would you please forgive me?"

For the first time, I came face-to-face with the prospect that I might never have the chance to receive his forgiveness—that Alex might have slipped away from us forever. Reeling from this new possibility, my body sank back into the chair, visibly defeated. But the chair could not stop my mind's cascading into a black abyss—my lowest point since this nightmare began.

It was this day, of all that followed the accident, that I gave in to my deepest fears. I embraced the apparent failure of the moment and allowed it to define the future. In so doing, I allowed myself to become devastated. With this latest report from the therapist, everything had taken on a darkened hue. I cried as much that day as I had on the day of the accident. Alex couldn't move, couldn't breathe on his own, couldn't speak, and couldn't swallow. If he couldn't think and understand, then in what sense was he really Alex?

Where had my faith gone? Why did I embrace doubt after so many victories? I guess I am a lot like Peter when Jesus told him to get out of the boat and walk on water, confident in Jesus one moment and focused on the waves—and sinking—the next. But even though I was giving the Giant Despair a temporary free pass in my mind, no one was giving up, including me.

The therapists were wonderful, soldiering on despite these setbacks. The speech therapist was particularly tenacious and gave me a lot of encouragement. Not too long after the negative news, she helped Alex develop three facial movements that gave us true hope. He could move the corner of his mouth on the right side of his face. We were able to establish with him that this expression meant the word *yes*. Puckered lips, we agreed with Alex, meant the word *no*. Alex's all-time favorite expression, however, was rolling his eyes, which took on a variety of meanings, depending on context. For example:

I don't know.

Your questions are bugging me.

My dad is a nut job.

And just about anything else from the massive realm of possibilities between yes and no.

Mirror Motivation

The growth of Alex's hair was keeping pace with the length of his hospital stay, so a friend of ours came down to give him a haircut.

Out of this most simple procedure, we learned something new about Alex. As the barber was working away, we suddenly realized that Alex

---

+++ Alex continues to become more aware. Each of the therapists is noting his daily progression. He drew a picture of an umbrella today (with help), and he is moving his eyes to "yes" and "no" cards as a foundation for his communication skills. Beth is learning to cath him, clean his G-tube, and work on the vent. My training begins Thursday a.m. at 9:00. . . .

We believe now that Alex can handle whoever wants to come to his room, so feel free to visit. Let's just try not to have too many people in the room at the same time so that he is not overwhelmed. Please remember that children are allowed to visit.

We heard from our pastor that electricity is back on and that the leak on our roof seems reasonably well maintained. I will go out to the house late tonight to make sure everything is ready for our family's return. Beth has some concerns about the stability of the roof. Please pray for wise decision making and safety for our family as we try to return home.

Leaving Alex's room is very difficult when he is awake now because he clearly understands that we are leaving him. . . . Alex, Beth, and I all cried tonight as we tried to learn to help Alex feel peaceful about his situation. What a blessing it is though that he is taking in, processing, and feeling again.

Thank you, God, for Your miraculous healing in our son.

PrayforAlex.com post by Kevin Malarkey on January 12, 2005 +++

---

had caught sight of himself in the mirror. This was the first time he'd seen himself since coming back to consciousness. Upon catching his image in the mirror, Alex immediately began attempting to make his facial muscles do what his mind wanted.

Alex stared intently into the mirror, doing battle with the recalcitrant muscles, his face twitching and eyes burning with determination. I watched quietly, but in my heart I was on the sidelines of this immense struggle jumping up and down, screaming at the top of my lungs, *Go Alex! Go Alex!*

This was the Alex I knew, the fighter, the child showing the initiative to take the tools he had and perfect his use of them. He was fighting for all he was worth with everything he had. He wasn't just lying there, giving up because of the obstacles he faced. He was being proactive, refusing to give in. I may have been quietly holding a mirror while sitting on the edge of his bed, but inside I was high-fiving everyone in the stadium: *Did you see that play? That's my son Alex. He's a winner!*

For two hours I held the mirror while Alex practiced all his moves—moving the corner of his mouth, puckering his lips, and rolling his eyes.

I sat watching, in awe of his determination, beaming with pride. There could be no mistake about it now. Alex, the one and only Alex we loved, was in there fighting to get out. Every doctor knows how imperative the will to fight is. Lose that, and it's all over. Several times we had asked ourselves if Alex possessed that vital drive. Now we had our answer, and it filled us with renewed energy to keep our minds and hearts in the game.

Before this moment, I hadn't realized how low my spirits had become. But no sooner did I watch my young warrior doing battle than the fight came back into me, too. In that incredible moment, my son became my hero and my inspiration. I was and am his father and mentor, but in that instant our relationship changed forever. It was then that I had the first inkling that Alex had a lot to teach me about courage, determination, and keeping up the fighting spirit.

Week by week Alex's command of his facial muscles grew. One of the early exercises was for him to blow into a straw. The therapist would attach the straw to a device that would move a small ball about twelve inches up a tube, toppling it to the ground. To help motivate Alex to keep at it, we put a little medicine cup of water on the top of the device and then asked for "volunteers" to put their heads near enough so that when Alex blew hard enough to topple the cup, the volunteer would be splashed with water. Watching that happen was all the encouragement Alex needed; soon he was blowing that straw for all he was worth.

Alex didn't remain satisfied with his progress for very long. He wasn't content to limit his ability to communicate to facial expressions. Now that this battle was won, the battle to push actual words out of his mouth was just beginning. People who sustain severe brain injuries must often learn to speak all over again. Alex was up for the challenge.

Starting from somewhere in his throat, each sound would make the torturous journey over his tongue and out his mouth. In the beginning, they were mostly earnest, garbled noises. He would work the sounds from throat and mouth the best he could, and we would spend the next five or ten minutes trying to decipher their meaning. Alex would then give the signal for *no* until we got it right. We were like linguists establishing the basis for communication in

+++ Alex continues to work hard in his therapy. The speech therapist is working on strengthening the muscles in his face, getting Alex to communicate with his eyes using cards and objects. . . . Alex continues to push out sounds, but they are difficult to understand. He was able to increase his volume a bit when asked to by the speech therapist. In all honesty, all three of us in the room thought that the word Alex was trying to say was *Jesus*.

I had a difficult time yesterday as I had conflicting emotions watching Alex. Everything he is doing is literally a miracle. He is much more aware, and he is trying so hard. At the same time, it is hard to believe that my brilliant little boy is struggling so hard to make a sound. I have wept on a couple of occasions as I see his pain and frustration. Strangely as it often is in life, progress leads to a more difficult and intense level of struggle.

PrayforAlex.com post by Kevin Malarkey on January 15, 2005 +++

an unknown tongue. It was like mining for precious gems, and we rejoiced over every single word.

As with anything worthwhile, the real work started after the fun of the new enterprise had worn off. As Alex tried to form words, we were both thrilled and frustrated. We wanted so badly to have a normal conversation with him, and he was working tirelessly to make that happen. We simply had to hang in there with him until we could figure out what it was he was trying to say. It could be frustrating for him, too, but Alex had nearly miraculous patience and determination. Even a six-year-old has complex thoughts, feelings, and reactions to share, and we wondered what was within him that might run deeper than a simple yes or no.

We all needed perseverance. In the middle of this effort, Beth came up with a brilliant idea that I, the psychotherapist of the household, could only admire. She proclaimed a rule against Alex's trying to communicate about anything he *couldn't* do. We would follow along and figure out what he was saying, but if we determined he was talking about an inability, we stopped and asked him to name three abilities. It was a page straight from my father's philosophy, and it set the tone for the kind of positive emotional attitude that Alex already had but vitally needed to maintain.

For so many months Alex hadn't seemed to know or care whether we were present. Now when we left the room, he would become visibly upset and had a whole arsenal of protest expressions at his disposal. We all need to be needed. Maybe that's why I loved that Alex would become upset when we stepped out of the room. After not knowing if he would ever come back, it was comforting that when he did, he needed me.

Angels in Rehab

What a joyous development it was when Alex came out of his coma, when he came back to us—a direct answer to the prayer of thousands, a direct blessing to his dad and mom. I was still riding high from this momentous occasion about two weeks later when I went to visit him one night. Arriving in his room, I found that Margaret, a new acquaintance from a local church, was there, having signed up on the prayer schedule.

Perhaps he was tired, perhaps discouraged—whatever the reason, Alex didn't want to answer the litany of yes/no questions that had

+++ Alex . . . demonstrated some skills that he has not mastered prior to today. He opened his mouth on command, he stuck out his tongue on command, he used his chin to press a lever and perform a task. He also demonstrated some connections between his cognitions, his emotions, and his physical movements.

The lack of the presence of most of these skills was discussed at a meeting [yesterday]. It seems that when medical staff meet and discuss what Alex cannot do, God likes to show up the next day and mix things up a bit. I have been concerned about Alex's motivational level, and he now has shown us that he can be highly motivated (he used his chin to move a lever that moved a toy for at least ten minutes). I have watched him struggle to use muscles in the right side of his face, and he used these muscles perfectly as he had his "smiling face" on for at least five to ten minutes. He has now demonstrated a full range of emotions.

God is waking up our son more each day, and Alex is responding like a warrior (David). He has been strong and courageous like Joshua. Most of all, though, he has been blessed by a loving God. We still wait for God to breathe breath back into Alex so that he may get rid of the ventilator. I still believe that this will happen soon.

Thank you for your prayers. Please continue to pray for us that we may honor God and conform to His character.

PrayforAlex.com post by Kevin Malarkey on January 20, 2005 +++

become the centerpiece of our interaction in those two weeks since he had regained consciousness. Margaret and I started talking about various aspects of the new reality, Alex conscious and interacting with us. These were such exciting times, filled with new hope.

Margaret happened to be talking when suddenly Alex's countenance dramatically changed. His mouth opened wider than I had ever seen it, and it remained open, something that had never happened before. At first, Alex stared straight up at the ceiling of his room, but then his eyes began darting round the room. He didn't look at Margaret or me again, which was highly unusual. When I would enter Alex's room, his eyes were normally fixed directly on me 90 percent of the time. This night was different. For the next two hours Alex looked at me only about 20 percent of the time. Something strange was happening.

I began asking Alex a series of questions, desperately attempting to figure out what was going on. It was exhausting. I asked him every question I could think of—at least a hundred. Just when I could think of nothing else to ask, it dawned on me: we might not be alone. After all, angels had visited before, when Alex's neck was healed.

"Alex, are there angels in the room here with us? Show me with your eyes."

An even bigger smile broke out across Alex's face as he looked at Margaret. When he smiled big, I knew the answer to my question was yes, but when he looked at Margaret, I was a little confused.

"Is Margaret an angel?"

Alex puckered his lips to indicate no.

"Okay, Alex, is the angel *behind* Margaret?"

Alex curled the corner of his mouth to say yes.

At first, Alex indicated that there were many angels in the room, but then most of them left until only three remained. To find out how many angels were present, I would offer numbers until I got a

+++ I told Kevin that had I not been there, but had just been reading the post, I probably would have doubted what had happened—not Kevin's honesty, but just maybe he was being a little too hopeful. Please understand when you read this that I'm someone who has to have things really proved to me. I probably would have stood behind Thomas for my turn to touch Jesus' nail-scarred hand.

I have been a Christian for thirty-two years, and I've never experienced what I experienced [that] night. For the first forty-five minutes Kevin was there he had Alex's undivided attention—which I understand is usual. Once Alex began to open his mouth wide and look around, the only time he focused on his dad was when we asked questions. Everything you've read in the two angels' messages happened, but I wish everyone reading this could have seen Alex's face. He was truly radiant.

Margaret Mokry +++

yes. Then things changed again. It seemed that Alex was trying to talk. We watched with great intensity as Alex struggled to form a word. Following an immense effort that visibly marshaled every fiber of his will, Alex said, "Mom"! Then, as if to ensure that the word wouldn't escape, he began to say it over and over again. My heart couldn't contain the joy of that moment of triumph. I had cried a lot up to this point, but I liked these tears much better.

Wait till I tell Beth, I thought. Then Alex moved his mouth to say another word. Now he was trying to say "Dad," but the *d* sound requires the tongue, an oral maneuver that was yet too difficult for him. But it was a great triumph nonetheless. Alex glowed while he talked about the angels, his yes answers indicated by huge smiles rather than moving the corner of his mouth like he normally did.

Alex saying his first word—was this why Alex's angels came? I believe it was. Does this sound strange? If it is hard for you to read this and believe, you should try typing it. Imagine how I feel. I come from a conservative evangelical context. These events are not part of my experience or background, but I can't deny or ignore that they took place.

I never saw an angel, but without the slightest doubt or hesitation, I am certain that I watched my child interacting with them. Margaret shares this conviction. It may sound crazy, but it did happen. I'll leave the explanations to the theologians.

From Alex
Angels Helping Me

I trust him with all my heart. He helps me, and my heart is filled with joy. I burst out in songs of thanksgiving.

PSALM 28:7

I had seen a lot of angels in Heaven, but that was when I wasn't in my body.

After two months I finally came out of my coma, but I couldn't talk. I knew what I wanted to say, but I couldn't say it. That was really hard.

I could pucker my lips to say no and curl the corner of my

mouth to say yes. I could also roll my eyes, which meant "I don't know." But that was all.

One night about two weeks after I came out of my coma, Daddy and another friend named Margaret were with me. I was tired and didn't feel like trying to answer questions, so Daddy and Margaret were just talking to each other.

Then something happened. I saw angels in my room. They were everywhere. That made me have a really huge smile. I never keep my mouth open for very long, but now I couldn't shut it.

I was so happy that the angels came, but there were so many of them, I was a little scared, too. Daddy had never seen me smile like that, and he tried to figure out what I was doing.

Daddy started asking me a whole lot of questions to try to understand. It took a long time, but finally Daddy said, "Alex, do you see angels?" I smiled even bigger, and then Daddy and Margaret knew there were angels in my room.

I couldn't stop looking at them. Then the angels started to help me.

Some of the angels put their hands on my chest and were helping me breathe. Other angels started to help me talk. I started to try to make words with my mouth and all of a sudden, I said "Mom." When that word came out, I was very happy and said it over and over. I then tried to form the word *Daddy*, but I couldn't make the word come out.

The angels could hear me talk, and they talked to me, encouraging me.

Before the accident

Alex, just before turning three, with his new-born best buddy, Aaron. The two brothers have always been inseparable.

ABOVE ▲

Taken two weeks before the accident, this is the last picture of Gracie, Aaron, and Alex all together and healthy. Sometimes I have a hard time remembering what it was like when Alex could walk. In those moments, I look at this picture.

RIGHT ▶

This would not be the last time Alex was like Superman. Several years later he would have the "Christopher Reeve surgery."

EXAMINER PHOTO BY BRIAN J. EVANS

The vehicle of Kevin L. Malarkey, 39, of 2109 County Road 57, Huntsville, sits along State Route 47 after it was struck Saturday by a vehicle operated by Emily Jill McCain, 23, of 112 N. Everett St., Apt. A, at the intersection of County Road 9. Mr. Malarkey's 6-year-old son was critically injured in the accident.

Boy critical after crash

Four others also injured in Saturday accident

\By THE EXAMINER STAFF

A 6-year-old Huntsville boy remained in critical condition this morning in the intensive care unit at Children's Hospital in Columbus after a crash Sunday afternoon.

William Alexander Malarkey, 2109 County Road 57, was flown by a MedFlight helicopter to the hospital, where deputies of the Logan County Sheriff's Office report he was on a life support system.

He was injured in a 1:35 p.m. wreck at the intersection of State Route 47 and County Road 9 in which his father, Kevin L. Malarkey, 39, turned in front of a car driven by Emily Jill McCain, 23, of 112 N. Everett St., Apt. A.

Mr. Malarkey was eastbound attempting to turn onto C.R. 9 and failed to see the westbound McCain car, which struck his car, forcing it into a ditch on the northwest corner of the intersection.

Mr. Malarkey, Ms. McCain and her two children, Zoe Madison Gingrey, 6, and Zander B. McCain, 1, were taken to Mary Rutan Hospital by Bellefontaine and Robinaugh squads for less serious injuries.

The father was ejected from the vehicle. There was conflicting information about which occupants of the vehicles were wearing seat belts or child restraints, but the report consistently indicated William was wearing a lap and shoulder belt.

The Bellefontaine Police Department also assisted at the scene.

ABOVE ▲

I remember seeing this story on an ICU computer a few weeks after the accident. It was surreal to read Alex's name in print while he was in a coma a few feet away from me, fighting for his life.

BELOW ▾

One of the worst moments of my life was getting into this ambulance while Alex was taking off in the chopper. I couldn't believe I had to be separated from my injured son.

ABOVE ▴

We don't know if this photo shows the actual helicopter used to save Alex, but we do know that MedFlight staff helped to save Alex's life through amazing care and heartfelt prayer.

◇ ◇

On the scene

This photo shows the deadly illusion of this road—it appeared wide open, but a hidden dip concealed the approaching car. I never saw it coming.

BELOW ▼

Christmas Day 2004—our family was together for the first time in almost six weeks. Although we didn't know what would happen to Alex, we were so grateful he was still with us that we couldn't help but rejoice.

ABOVE ▲

Still in a coma, Alex sits in his wheelchair while wearing a back brace. (You can see "Doggie," Alex's favorite stuffed companion, sitting on his lap. Doggie has been through many surgeries with Alex and has even ridden in the ambulance.)

Recovery

RIGHT ►

Our license plate speaks for itself. Alex believes he will walk again—and so do I.

BELOW ▼

This is the painting described in chapter 6. A friend had a vision of three angels hovering over Alex. Weeks later, we found that another woman (a complete stranger to the first) had painted this picture at the same time.

ABOVE ▲

I was blown away when I saw this image. Why? Read chapter 3 for the full story.

ABOVE ▲

I still tear up when I look at this picture. It was the first time I was able to finally hold Alex in my arms again. A very, very good day.

◄ LEFT

Friends surprised us by decorating our home for Alex's arrival. He came home joyfully with a nurse, a respiratory therapist, two EMTs, and two nervous parents . . . but he would go back to the hospital only days later.

Coming home

Alex getting fitted for his wheelchair, which he could operate himself by moving his chin.

To keep his body in motion, Alex walks in his Hoyer lift, he goes on the treadmill, he even goes swimming. He is totally fearless.

Our new normal

Whether it's a sleepover in the church gym or football practice with our hero, Coach Jim Tressel, it takes many volunteers, many vehicles, and many hours to get Alex anywhere—but he's unquestionably worth it.

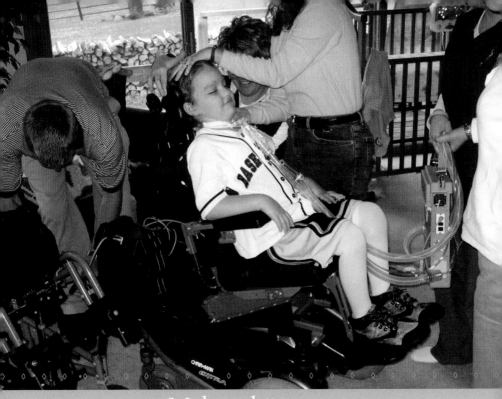

Making history

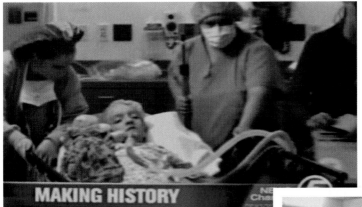

BELOW ▼

World-renowned surgeon Dr. Raymond Onders performed the groundbreaking procedure. He treated Alex with unbelievable personal attention and remains a friend to our family.

ABOVE ▲

In 2009, Alex made international news as the first child ever to undergo the surgery made famous by actor Christopher Reeve.

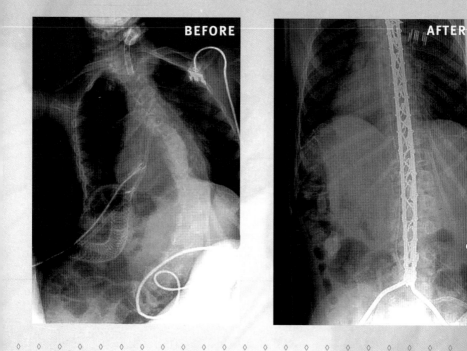

BEFORE **AFTER**

Straight ahead

ABOVE ▲

These "before and after" X-rays are from another surgery Alex had in 2009. This procedure straightened his spine, which had been curved at an 89-degree angle.

BELOW ▼

For Beth and me, our kids—Aaron, Alex, Gracie, and Ryan—are the joy of our life. Maybe this isn't your traditional family photo, but it's full of happiness and love. Please don't feel bad for us . . . because we don't.

CHAPTER 7

HOMECOMINGS

"Do you think I should turn this car around and
lead the ambulance right back where we came
from? Are we making a huge mistake?"

IT HAD BEEN several months since Columbus Children's had become
our home away from home. The ministry of God's people had kept
our lives from completely unraveling, and we were deeply grateful.
But by this time, home was where we needed to be. The prospect
of taking Alex home required three things. He had to be stable and
strong; Beth and I had to be ready (knowledgeable enough) to care
for him; and our house had to be ready to shelter us.

I continued to believe that Alex would breathe on his own before
he left that hospital. It didn't happen. A new trach tube helped with
the discomfort Alex was feeling with the breathing equipment, but
he really wanted to be free of it. He was also becoming stiff and
needed stretching to keep his body limber.

Throughout all this, Alex never lost his sense of humor, which he had brought with him out of his coma. He playfully dubbed one of his assistants "Jane the Pain."

Angels, he assured us, continued to come and go. When the pastor was there praying for him, for example, four were present, though only Alex could see or hear them. (Miles away, we had eight angels of our own up on the roof of our house, but they were the visible and noisy type. We were grateful for their "surgery" on our ailing home.)

After months of living half our lives in the hospital and trying to get everything else done in a parallel universe, Beth and I were wearing down, and our relationship had developed some rough edges. There were many times I wished I could take back sharp words and bad attitudes. I know Beth felt the same. The truth is, at times we exhibited our worst sides to each other, often in earshot of others. We aren't proud of our behavior, but an honest account of these times mustn't gloss over the trauma our marriage sustained in the midst of everything else. There were too many demands: caring for Alex, supplying love and physical needs for three other children, getting our house repaired, resuming my business—we knew we couldn't maintain such a schedule forever. Several times we recommitted ourselves to supporting and leaning on each other, getting enough sleep, and depending upon the prayers of our many supporters.

Stressed but Blessed

In the last days at Children's Hospital, tensions heightened. Sleep was evasive. We were given a crash course in caring for our son, a quadriplegic on a respirator, and felt inadequately prepared for the challenge. These desperate hours pushed us to the limit and, again, we failed to live up to our ideals of what a Christian marriage should be. Not to make excuses for our sin. But in retrospect we believe we took on too much too soon.

+++ There have been nights and weeks and days when my body was so spent I did not know how I could function, move, or breathe. There have been assaults to my character, my spirituality, my relationship with Jesus. There has been nothing spared to try to stop me. The cool thing is, not only did God give me a compassionate heart so that I hurt when other people hurt, but He also gave me stubbornness— in a good way. He knows I will not stop.

I tell people, "I wish I could take credit for some of this, but I can't." I can only explain it as Him. I recognize His supernatural strength, wisdom, knowledge, and understanding all the time. I have learned to cling to the Savior.

Beth Malarkey, Alex's mom +++

Our Internet correspondents thought we'd dropped off the face of the earth. Whenever we got home, we collapsed into bed, only to get up and move on to the next high-priority task after just a few precious hours of sleep. Beth was feeling totally overwhelmed, and I felt helpless in trying to support and encourage her—my own hands were full at the same time. I also worried that I was losing track of my other three children because there simply weren't enough hours in the day to attend to all my responsibilities.

In those final days at the hospital, Alex was learning to work with computers by himself, and not surprisingly he was very excited by the opportunity. He called the computer Alex 2 and operated it with a switch on his face. He could also use facial muscles to pilot a motorized wheelchair around the hospital. Reports soon filtered back to us that he was wreaking vengeance on Jane the Pain and other personnel, running them down in the hallways.

His attitude continued to amaze everyone. He thought his MRI was fun. He even got the nurses to take him down to the X-ray lab and convinced the technicians to take X-rays of two of his stuffed animals. He showed a gung-ho attitude about the wheelchair and every other new challenge introduced into his world. He labored tirelessly to regain the ability to talk. Everyone who saw Alex strive and fight for every inch of ground was encouraged, including his parents.

During this time, however, Alex began to feel some pain for what he had lost. After prayer one night, he told us he wished he could ride his bike. As his limbs grew stiffer, his memory grew more supple, bringing back all the things he used to do—the trees he once climbed, the games he played, and the bike he rode. His previous, little-boy life gradually came back into focus, only to remind him of what was now beyond his grasp.

The centerpiece of the care regimen Beth and I needed to master was changing Alex's tracheotomy tube. It was a complex, frightening task at first, but we were soon doing it without a hitch.

Whenever we found ourselves at our wits' end, God was there waiting to show us a bigger picture, to reveal His plans to us. He humbled us many times, demonstrating how much He loved us, how much He had blessed us.

While Alex was seeing angels in the hospital, we were experiencing God's angels of a different kind. Eight men worked tirelessly to rebuild our roof better than it was when the tree smashed it. Other volunteers worked to repair problems we had discovered in our new home since the accident. A complete (and very expensive) water filtration system was installed. God's angel contractors logged countless hours of work for plumbing, vents, and other essential functions in the house.

A donor paid $1,500 for a special mattress that Alex needed. Then, when the owner of the mattress company read about it on our Web site, he called the donor, got his address, and mailed the check back. Someone else supplied us with new appliances.

+++

We are weary, but we are fighting that others may see God (even though at times we hardly resemble disciples of Christ). . . . God is our strength, but you are His hands and feet.

PrayforAlex.com
post by Kevin Malarkey
on December 10, 2004

I've only touched the very tip of the iceberg. God's supplying our needs became so commonplace that we were in danger of taking for granted all that He was doing through His people to meet our needs and show the love that could grow among His children. As the Bible says, "Your love for one another will prove to the world that you are my disciples" (John 13:35).

The day approached for Alex's return home. The house was ready, but were we? We certainly didn't feel like it. With baby Ryan in tow, Beth drove to the hospital for the final meeting with the staff on February 14, 2005. I kept up via teleconference as I took care of Gracie and Aaron at home. At this point, there was nothing that worried me more than Beth's state of mind. She was exhausted mentally, physically, and emotionally, and I worried that through my impatience and insensitivity, I might be contributing to her struggle rather than alleviating it.

Alex would be coming home by ambulance the next morning. He was so excited he could almost have floated home. Instead of waiting for family members to come visit him, he would be with us all the time. When I reminded Alex that he would see his dog, Sadie, for the first time in three months, a huge smile broke out across his face.

Everyone was ecstatic that Alex was coming home, but despite our preparation, we felt as if we weren't even close to ready for his arrival.

Beth Hears about Heaven

As nurses came in and out of the room, Beth changed Alex's trach tube, with myriad details swirling in her already overburdened mind. Alex waited until Beth finished and then indicated that he wanted to be alone with Mommy and baby Ryan. The hospital staff respectfully left the room and shut the door. *What is on Alex's mind?* Beth wondered as she cuddled with him. Alex was at the stage when he could only form words with his mouth and make a faint whisper. Beth leaned in and listened. Alex mouthed, "I want to tell you about the accident."

"Okay, honey, what do you want to tell me?"

Beth's voice was even, but her spirit was startled. This was the last topic she expected Alex to talk about in the moments prior to going home. And it was the first time Alex had spoken to us about the day of the accident.

"Jesus came and got me from the car and kept me close to Him the whole time. I was above my body, watching everyone work on me. I was safe. Jesus kept talking to me, telling me I was going to be okay, so I was never afraid."

At this, a radiant smile bathed Alex's face. He had wanted so long to share his experience and was now gaining the ability to form the words with his mouth, even if he couldn't get much sound out of his lips.

"What else did you see?"

"I saw Daddy taken out of the car. The angels set him down in the ditch."

Beth understood what Alex meant by "taken out." He was saying that his daddy was never thrown from the car, nor had he wandered out in a daze. Angels had literally carried his body to a safe place.

"Then I saw Daddy yelling my name: 'Alex! Alex! Alex!' Daddy didn't know where I was, and he was worried about me."

"Did that make you sad, honey?"

"No. I wasn't sad. I was with Jesus. Then lots more firemen came. One fireman brought Daddy his phone, and I saw him make a call."

Beth's mind raced back to the moment of that call. Humanly speaking, Alex had no way of knowing about it.

"Another fireman put something in my mouth to help me breathe. A nurse helped me in the car. The firemen took me out of the car and put me on a flat board. They cut my shirt off. It was my plaid shirt. They took off my shoes, too. Daddy went over to the helicopter to talk with the man in the blue suit."

"Alex, do you mean an orange suit? I think that's what he may have been wearing."

"No, Mommy. It was a blue suit!"

This would have been the man from MedFlight, the air medical transport group that had provided the helicopter. Later Beth asked me about the uniform, because when Dave had spoken to her at the hospital, she was sure he was in an orange suit. But I told her that Alex was right on the money—it was indeed blue.

"I saw the helicopter man bend over me and pray for me. Then they also put Daddy on a flat board before they put him in the ambulance. They cut off his clothes, too."

All of this was true, and he had no way to know any of it. He had been unconscious from soon after the accident, and by the time the medical personnel were tending to me, he was already in the helicopter, heading to Children's Hospital.

"Honey, tell me where you went," Beth continued.

"Mommy, I was with Jesus, but my body, down under me, was not breathing. But Jesus said, 'You shouldn't worry. You are going to breathe again.'"

"Did He say when?"

"No, He didn't."

"What about angels?"

"They were there too."

"Do you remember anything else, honey?"

"My Barneys were everywhere!"

Beth laughed. We had almost forgotten about the old cloths he carried around instead of a security blanket. Just as he said, the Barneys had been spread across the scene.

"And I remember the room where they worked on me when I got to the hospital. There were many people. Maybe . . . twenty people? They were all helping to work on me. They all said how bad I was hurt. They were very sad."

"Did that make you afraid?"

"No. I was never afraid as long as Jesus was with me. Jesus told me I should tell you all about it. "

"Thanks, honey. I'm really glad you did."

Beth took a moment to reflect on this amazing conversation and what had led up to it. With too much to do at home, she had not intended to come to the meeting today. She was already at the end of her rope in every conceivable way, and with Alex coming home, life was not going to grow simpler. The plan was for her to stay home and for me to come to the meeting, but we changed our minds at the last minute . . . or, rather, God changed the plan. Jesus had wanted Beth there. Jesus had a message for her through her son Alex. *Okay, Lord*, she thought. *You have my attention. I'm listening.*

She had begun that morning feeling overwhelmed, wondering how she could keep going. Now it was revealed so clearly through the mouthed words of a child that God was still in control. His grace was sufficient. Alex had never been afraid because he had been sitting with Jesus. Shouldn't she be resting in Jesus too? The message couldn't be more direct. In the quietness of that room, Beth gave silent thanks to God. And as in this moment with Alex, we have found over and over that when we are desperate for God, He is everywhere to be found.

Later that day, I arrived at the hospital room to remove Alex's last few possessions. As I did, a little voice—a beautiful, magical, wonderful little voice—from the bed fell on my ears.

"Dad."

Joy surged through my heart as I whirled around to look into Alex's ecstatic, smiling face. He had struggled so hard to say my name a few days earlier, and now he said it with perfect clarity hours before we were set to leave the hospital. Tears of happiness ran freely down my face. Just as Alex found his voice, I lost mine. But that didn't stop me from making a series of incoherent phone calls, trying to tell everyone what had just happened.

It was three months to the day since I'd last heard him say a word to me from the backseat of our car.

Was it a going-away present or a homecoming gift?

All I could think was, *Thank you, Lord! Thank you so much.*

Home and Away

The next morning I was back at the hospital. Since we had virtually lived at Children's for the past three months, the paraphernalia of life had grown to astounding proportions. Several vanloads were needed to make Alex's move from hospital to home—and that was just our stuff! The real challenge was transporting Alex by ambulance. Beth and the other three children waited at the house while Alex and I stood by at the hospital. It says in the Bible that God will be with us whenever we go through deep waters, supplying the grace we need. Perhaps that's why I didn't know that this was only the first of twelve ambulance trips that Alex and I would take in the next few months. Had I known it the day we brought him home that first time, my heart would have broken. In my mind, as I drove toward home with Alex's ambulance following, we were *going home for good.*

The prospect of ending the exhausting back-and-forth commute was an immense relief, but even so, it is difficult to convey to the uninitiated the physical, emotional, and relational strain of providing acute care 24-7. Unless you've been in the throes of it, imagining it won't provide the full picture. Like a pencil that has spent too much time in the sharpener, Beth and I were so low by this time that all we could manage was sheer survival. Just keeping the family functioning required more than we had to give, but we had to (and willingly did) give it. Consequently, Beth and I had nothing left for each other. I would never consider divorce, yet I have no difficulty understanding why marriages not based on the Rock but caught up in traumatic circumstances end up there.

We were highly anxious, to say the least, about being directly responsible for Alex's care in our home, with the "backup" miles away. We had so many questions. What would it be like caring for Alex under our own roof? Could we manage the task, even with the assistance of visiting nurses? What if a medical emergency arose? Then there were questions about Alex. Just how long was his youthful spirit going to hold up? He'd shown so much heart, such a positive attitude, and a fighting spirit, too. He simply had no surrendering within him. How many of us would have yielded to despair after waking up to paralysis and a breathing machine? But was there a limit? Could we, as his caregivers, follow his lead and keep from becoming discouraging influences ourselves? Sometimes it seemed as if *he* was the one keeping *our* spirits up.

In the midst of our flesh's weakness, God had never been more present in our lives, and I did thank and praise Him. But there were so many more needs. I had to confess a great deal of fear and apprehension about the future. I wanted badly for this to work and to prove wrong all the people who said that we or Alex couldn't handle home care. Deep down, though, I wondered if we were doing the right thing.

Beth was struggling as much as I was. She really needed the Lord's strength and courage, and she needed her husband's undergirding support. She was worried about the nursing situation, which was complicated to set up and manage. Even though Beth and I are naturally independent, we had become dependent on skilled medical assistants. They had become our security blanket. There had been plenty of minor emergencies during the hospital stay. What would we do during a "minor" emergency if the trained nursing staff happened to be absent? With Alex on a ventilator, we were constantly mindful of the urgency of his next breath. A few moments of malfunction could mean his death. This thought alone took a constant toll on our emotions.

So this was a gargantuan step. How many times we had earnestly prayed for this day, this homecoming—but as they say, be careful what you pray for. What we gained by being together again as a family we lost in medical skill and immediate professional help.

I continued along the highway toward home with the ambulance carrying Alex a few hundred feet behind. The homecoming nursing arrangement still hadn't been finalized. Couldn't these people get their schedules straight? Like most people, even on a good, stress-free day, I have a low threshold for red tape and bureaucracy. This day, with Alex coming home, assuming the full responsibility for his care . . . *Help me to chill out, Lord.*

I sighed and called another number—a friend who was a nurse. After confessing my doubts and growing anxiety, I asked, "Do you think I should turn this car around and lead the ambulance right back where we came from? Are we making a huge mistake? Maybe we're just not ready. Tell me what you really think."

She encouraged me to hang in there, and within a few minutes, I was finally heading up our lengthy driveway. Rounding the last corner, I saw Beth, holding baby Ryan, and Aaron and Gracie, jumping up and down, waving me in. Their glowing faces were just what my heart needed. In those few moments, the worst of the anxiety melted away. I had so much to be thankful for: my wife, my children, and Alex awake and home, mind and spirit intact. Yes, indeed, much to give thanks for.

I parked near the house and was quickly mobbed, but the main attraction soon commanded everyone's attention. As Alex, strapped to a gurney, was rolled down a ramp, tears ran down our faces. Somehow Alex's arrival punctuated the end of something and the start of something more. We hadn't anticipated our response to his arrival and couldn't stop crying. It's funny how such a moment can catch you off guard. The presence of paramedics, a respiratory therapist, and other medical personnel soon refocused our attention on the work of moving Alex and all the medical equipment into the house.

Home but Not Alone

We had decorated the walls with brightly colored banners welcoming Alex. Beth had been putting in long hours getting the house ready, tidying the rooms for the constant flow of visitors, and making space for all the medical equipment that would need to be installed. Meanwhile, of course, she had three small children to watch—two of them quite active.

Meals came flooding in like manna from Heaven. The wonderful people of the church did what God's people seem to do with excellence: the ministry of the covered dish. They had an organized plan for making sure Beth could at least avoid laboring over a hot stove.

Two men showed up to assemble the swing set, which still sat in its boxes these many months since we'd bought the house. And that's the way tasks would be accomplished around the house for a long time. Whenever there was a job to do, two or more men would show up and get it done for us. Our pastor was a regular visitor, as were so many others who wanted to pray with us and offer love and encouragement. One thing we definitely didn't have to cope with was loneliness. We felt incredible support, locally and from distant parts.

Other medical professionals began arriving at regular intervals. There was an occupational therapist, a physical therapist, a speech therapist, a respiratory therapist, and a cadre of nurses working twelve-hour shifts in our home, generally six days each week. In addition, their supervisor dropped in occasionally to make sure everything was going smoothly and to make suggestions. All of these people loved Alex, and he returned their affection and responded to their instructions with superhuman effort. At least for the immediate future, we wouldn't be alone. But even with all this help, the hospital seemed light-years away.

The front porch became filled with strange boxes as the UPS truck dropped off new medical supplies virtually every day. The hospital had been our home for three months; now our home was becoming a hospital.

We could never have envisioned how many people would come and go each day. We all but needed to install a parking deck by the side of the house. Even when we were an ordinary family with four healthy children, our home had seemed quiet compared to the hustle and bustle that was now our daily environment. We were thankful for every visitor and every new medical device, however, because we knew these things made Alex's life better.

Our challenge was to somehow maintain an intimate family circle and be the parents that all four of our children needed. Just having one-on-one time with each child required tremendous awareness and creativity. Time for Beth and me as a married couple—well, that was something of a distant memory. Maybe someday there would be a time when we could take off, go somewhere, and attend to nothing in the world other than nurturing our love and commitment. It was hard to imagine when that day might be.

By the time Beth and I hit our bed on the night of Alex's homecoming, we were utterly spent. Alex was settled down, our children were in bed, the respirators and other machinery were humming, and a nurse was on duty. Tomorrow would be a little less frenzied, wouldn't it?

Home and Hearth

The following day I rose from bed immediately feeling the pull of the computer. How had the homecoming gone? Our Internet friends would be eager to hear. Just as I was pressing the power button to log on, Alex's faint but somehow insistent voice broke the morning stillness.

"Daddy?"

Though Alex was "speaking" to us regularly, it wasn't always audible. He carefully mouthed every word he wanted to say, working his facial muscles as vigorously as he possibly could. Sometimes there was a little squeak of a voice, sometimes nothing.

I immediately gave him all my attention. He'd been so delighted to be home again, and what he wanted now was for me to start a fire in the hearth. For him, that was one of the exciting features of the new house, something you certainly couldn't get at a hospital. For months his spirit had been animated by the hope of seeing his dog again, enjoying a fire, and being with his siblings more often. I wheeled him into the family room, where he sat for several hours, just basking in the coziness of his own home. The moment was perfect, because the morning sun revealed five inches of snow on the ground. That put a big smile on Alex's face.

Now, as he sat in the family room and enjoyed the crackling fire, he could look through the window and see snow collecting on tree branches and birds at the feeder. These were things he loved, and there had been a time when we'd wondered if he would ever open his eyes again to such simple joys. Some would expect him to be looking out at the snow with bitterness, remembering how he had played in it the previous winter. But that simply wasn't Alex. He had never seemed so pleased.

Viktor Frankl, author of *Man's Search for Meaning*, was a survivor of the Nazi prison camps. He had observed the various ways in which men and women respond to suffering, and he wrote, "Everything can be taken from a man but one thing: the last of the human freedoms—to choose one's attitude in any given set of circumstances, to choose one's own way."

Alex was living proof of that. This is why I have often said that at a certain point, Alex became my mentor, my coach for the right attitude in life. If such a little guy can be so resilient through terrible circumstances, then I know that I can face nearly anything. What I have seen in my son is a living demonstration of childlike faith, demonstrating the truth of what the Scriptures say:

> *Can anything ever separate us from Christ's love? Does it mean he no longer loves us if we have trouble or calamity, or are persecuted, or hungry, or destitute, or in danger, or threatened with death? . . . No, despite all these things, overwhelming victory is ours through Christ, who loved us. And I am convinced that nothing can ever separate us from God's love. Neither death nor life, neither angels*

nor demons, neither our fears for today nor our worries about tomorrow—not even the powers of hell can separate us from God's love. No power in the sky above or in the earth below—indeed, nothing in all creation will ever be able to separate us from the love of God that is revealed in Christ Jesus our Lord.

(ROMANS 8:35, 37-39)

A Startling Conversation

During the quieter moments, Alex began to talk more frequently about the things that had occurred while he was away from us. For the first time, I began to suspect that my son had actually died at the accident scene. That possibility fit both the kind of injury he'd suffered as well as the kind of trip he professed to have had—a journey to Heaven itself. In addition, as the days went on, Alex was more insistent about his story. A fabricated account would have become inconsistent and eventually faded. Alex's narrative, though, was taking on more substance.

Early on, we didn't expect Alex to remember anything about the accident. But one of my greatest fears was that his memory would be gone altogether or, at best, be erratic. This fear surged almost as soon as Alex regained the ability to form sentences. As soon as he could get the words out, he asked me repeatedly, "Are you my dad?"

My facial expression didn't change, but when I heard those words, my heart instantly began to ache, as if I had been rejected in some fundamental way. It wasn't rational, I know, but when your boy wonders who you are, trust me, logic is no match for raw emotions.

Alex gradually became more adept at speaking, and conversations with him became very close to what we all consider ordinary. One of the earliest fluent conversations went like this:

"Are you my dad?"

"Yes, Alex, I'm Daddy."

"Are you sure you're my dad?"

"Yes, Alex, it's me."

"Because my daddy was killed in a car accident," he said. "You look like him, but my daddy's in Heaven."

"Alex, I was in a car accident with you," I explained, puzzled by his statement. "I was thrown out of the car, but I did not die."

"I'm sorry about the accident, Daddy."

"Me too, Alex, but it will be okay, buddy. God will get us through this."

"Daddy, the accident was my fault."

"No, Alex. I pulled in front of a car . . ."

"But I saw the car and didn't tell you. I asked a question and made you turn around. You didn't see the car."

"Alex, I'm the one who has wanted to say I'm sorry. I've been waiting to ask your forgiveness for three months. I almost got you killed!"

"Really, Daddy? I thought it was my fault. The devil told me I was to blame."

My heart was unbearably full as I heard these words. Had he been carrying these recollections all this time? Had he been laboring under a delusion of guilt these many weeks?

"No, Alex. I'm the one who caused the accident. Don't believe a word of what the devil says. You did not cause this accident. I did. Alex, will you please forgive me?"

"Yes, Daddy. I love you."

"Thank you, Alex. I love you more than anything."

As Alex's powers of speech grew, we began to sense that something far more than a mere coma had taken place over the course of the last few months. Alex began to relate to us details of an extended visit to Heaven. So many supernatural things had already happened that miracles were no longer surprising to us. We were thankful and grateful for every divine intervention, but Alex had begun talking about things far beyond anything we had yet experienced.

As a licensed clinical counselor, I knew exactly what the doctors would say about all this. They would attribute it to dreaming and a child's imagination, perhaps even hallucinations due to brain trauma. We all know that many people wake up after near-death experiences and have compelling stories to tell. Frankly, early on I didn't know what to make of what Alex was telling us either. The more pragmatic, "educated" part of me thought, *Maybe he* does *have brain damage; maybe he* is *imagining things.*

But we were three months into a supernatural adventure. We had never been more attuned to the work of the Lord or more conscious of spiritual warfare. Never had we depended so heavily on a God who intervenes in life. My trained skepticism had been tempered by the miracles I had witnessed. If Alex said he'd seen the devil, I was ready to listen with an open mind. Who knew what his experiences had been during this amazing ride? Ours had certainly been unbelievable enough. I realized the problem wasn't Alex; the problem was me and my inability to believe what I said I believed.

In bits and pieces, Alex's cohesive story of Heaven and angels began to emerge. I listened to these things with wonder. The picture came together slowly but fully and always consistently. "Alex," I asked, "what did it feel like to move back into your body after being out of it for a while? That must have felt very strange."

He only squinted his eyes and formed the word "Ouch!"

I never asked leading questions. For example, I didn't say, "Was

Heaven white, like in the pictures?" Or "Did the angels have wings?" Every piece of information was something that Alex volunteered.

Over time, Alex shared more and more information. Since I don't have a charismatic background, all of this is new territory to me. I don't have a theological box to put it in. It is a reality that has invaded our lives.

Crisis

The nurses were in and out in a more sporadic way than we might have expected, but things were working out. For the first couple of days after Alex came home, Beth and I felt comfortable caring for him during those times when we were by ourselves.

Then, on that third day, Alex seemed to be having a rough go of it. We just couldn't make him comfortable. As the afternoon wore on, he began struggling for breath. The nurse helped to clear his airway, which made things better for a short time. Then he began struggling again. Next his body temperature plunged to a dangerous ninety-one; his heart rate hovered in the mid-sixties. A mucous buildup had developed in his throat, obstructing the trachea. This problem had to be dealt with immediately, but before we were able to clear the obstruction, Alex grew drowsy, unresponsive, and increasingly pale.

We couldn't handle this crisis, even with the nurse close at hand, and time was fast slipping away. Our only option was to call 911. From the start, I had had my secret doubts about the wisdom of our providing all of Alex's care at home. As we waited for help to arrive, I couldn't help but think, *Maybe this is confirmation Alex's situation is too complicated and dangerous to handle at home.*

The ambulance arrived, though not in a particularly speedy

manner. Thank goodness the professionals were there. The paramedics quickly trooped through the house to Alex's room, but stopped upon entering. Looking around at all the medical equipment, the head paramedic asked, "What do you want us to do?" Clearly, they didn't know what to do with someone on a ventilator.

"What do you mean, 'What do I want you to do?' I called in and told the dispatcher my son is on a vent and can't breathe, his temperature is dangerously low, and he's lethargic. If I knew you would ask me that question when you arrived, I wouldn't have called 911."

It was a tense moment, and everything—the life of my son—was on the line. The paramedics had no real answers other than to take Alex to the hospital, so they began wheeling him out. The visiting nurse and I accompanied the ambulance to the facility, while Beth stayed home with the little ones.

At the small local hospital, the doctors and other medical personnel tried their best, but it was soon obvious that they, too,

+++

Please pray for protection of Alex and [for] guidance. I know that he is in God's hands and will be okay, but it is challenging to be in a system where you feel like you know more than the people you are relying on. Please know that Alex is in really good spirits. God is in control.

PrayforAlex.com
post by Kevin Malarkey
on February 17, 2005

lacked the expertise to handle Alex's situation. It seemed that we knew more about our son's condition than these folks did. Suddenly we were the experts—we took the lead, and the doctors and nurses watched us carefully. I took on Alex's care myself, since I knew best how to do it.

To begin with, he was borderline hypothermic and needed to be warmed immediately. We covered him with blankets to increase his body temperature. I fed him through the G-tube in his stomach, monitored the ventilator, and did all the little things we had learned to help keep my son stable. None of this is intended to reflect poorly on the local hospital. We were a bit surprised by how little help they were prepared to give, but we found out that this is common in smaller hospitals. Alex's situation was such an acute and specialized one that it required the care that only a larger facility could provide. It wasn't until evening that we got permission to transfer Alex to Children's Hospital.

A Total Failure?

At the local hospital I watched Alex's vital signs like a hawk, anxiety coursing through me. I prayed constantly for mercy and help throughout that evening, which I thought would never end. Harrowing—there's no other word to describe the feeling of watching your son attempt to breathe, knowing there's nothing you can do but wait.

The ambulance to take Alex to Children's arrived. What a relief it was to finally get Alex the help he so desperately needed, but on another level, it felt like total failure. For weeks we had set our eyes on the big day when Alex would come home "for good." We'd built it up, mounted banners, fixed up the house with ramps and equipment, and managed to hold everything together for a grand total of three days. Now we had bounced right back to the place we had convinced ourselves we'd left forever.

On five more occasions during the next year, we would move back and forth between home and the respiratory unit at Children's. The stability we had sought eluded us. No matter how many times we told ourselves we were fortunate to have our son alive, we still succumbed to feelings of discouragement and, at times, even despair.

Physical exhaustion battered our hope. Many times we were too exhausted even to pray. Thank God for the prayers of the saints! They sustained us when putting one foot in front of the other was all we could do. There were many times Beth and I were little more than walking bundles of frayed nerves. Because of this, it was all the more surprising to see how many people were continuing to look at us as sources of spiritual inspiration—models of living faith. There was no shortage of talk that set us up as heroes or martyrs, profiles in courage. Why didn't other people seem to notice how stressed, moody, and unpleasant we could be? I could only hope these people figured out the real truth.

Please hear me when I say that our ability to hang in there had nothing to do with our strength, our faith, or any positive attribute of our own. As a matter of fact, these circumstances only humbled us. They showed us not our strengths, but our vast weaknesses; not our faith, but our faithlessness. Courage? We had never needed it more. We lived in fear of what the future might hold for Alex.

This wasn't about our strength; it was about God's. He was the only reason we had come this far without giving in to utter despair. We've heard about many crises that have destroyed marriages and families. I'm told that when a child dies, the parents very often end up getting a divorce. We struggled with the bad times, and we were forced into absolute dependence upon God, the only refuge we had, because we knew we weren't strong enough in ourselves to weather such a storm.

Every time we were tempted to give up or to give in, every time we were at the last tiny strand of the end of our rope, God would send human angels of comfort, or He would do something miraculous in Alex's life. The Lord constantly reminded us of His presence, unlimited power, and gracious love, while the situation itself reminded us of our limitations and weaknesses. On top of all this, the ever-responsive human angels of comfort were often the very people who professed great inspiration through our story! We were the ones who needed to be applauding them. They were the healing hands of God in our lives over and over. How could we possibly have made it through each day without them?

Most couples have the luxury of working out the kinks of their relationship in privacy, but we were living our lives in the waiting room of Children's Hospital and in the midst of a home that had become Grand Central. I might snap at Beth or some medical helper, or she might be exasperated with me, and then we'd feel doubly guilty—not only had we been rough on each other, but we'd aired our frustrations in public. We had presented a poor testimony of God's goodness. Many of these times our children were present as well. Quarreling in front of children is never a good thing, but they were right in front of us almost all the time.

It simply couldn't be helped, given the constant stress level, unless we really became the perfected saints people thought we were. That wasn't going to happen; we were ordinary people placed in an extraordinary situation, but blessed by a God who supplies our needs beyond all expectations. I only hope that in the final analysis, people saw much more of God than us in this situation. I know they had to see the anger I felt so often—never directed at the Lord, but sometimes at the doctors or at Beth. In the heat of the moment, I made statements to her that I would love to take back.

The Pressure Cooker

I'd love to forget more than a few instances when I snapped at others. One involved an argument with one of the doctors. I was deeply concerned because Alex was struggling to breathe, even on the vent. It was so frustrating to see that his lungs kept filling up with mucus, blocking the air he desperately needed. Couldn't something be done to keep the stuff from flowing? The doctors were convinced that it was an anxiety problem. They wanted to administer an anti-anxiety medication to Alex.

They got the diagnosis right but the patient wrong. I was the one who needed the prescription, particularly after hearing their prognosis. I knew Alex's problems were not emotionally based. I was furious, and the more the staff kept making that suggestion, the angrier I grew. What bothered me most was that Alex had been a model of courage and calmness all along. Yet here the doctors were claiming his state of mind was causing what were clearly physical problems.

With my emotional barometer surging, I stepped up to the doctor until we were in each other's faces. I'm six-foot-two and weigh 220 pounds, and I'm sure I can be an imposing presence when I lose my cool. The doctor was as stubborn as I was, insisting that Alex needed to be on anxiety meds. It was a bad combination. I finally blew a gasket. "Perhaps I should knock you on your rear end and then start jumping up and down on your chest so you can understand how it feels not to be able to breathe!" I shouted. "But you won't have to worry about breathing because I'll get you an anti-anxiety medication! Giving my son anti-anxiety meds may help his anxiety, but it won't help him breathe past the mucous clog covering part of his trachea!"

Believe me, it's hard to relate this episode from my past. Part of me would rather you listen to those who painted us as spiritual giants. But of course, that would be far from honest. This is a non-fiction book, and it tells a very true story. I want you to know that there's nothing at all special about me, and plenty inside me that God still needs to fix up. I'm very much a work in progress when it comes to being conformed to the image of Christ, the goal for all of us as believers. But as I work on this book, I always keep in mind Alex's reluctance to tell his story. His fear is that people will admire the human beings in the narrative, including himself, rather than the only One who should truly impress them.

Days of Worship

As if our local church hadn't already done more than enough, they decided to do something more—a Sunday-morning service dedicated to Alex. What an honor that was, a chance to magnify the Lord through the amazing things He was doing for our son. The best part, of course, was that Alex was able to be there and to enjoy every moment of it.

After we watched a brief video that told his story, I wheeled Alex down the center aisle. You can imagine what happened then—everyone jumped to their feet. Alex got a raucous standing ovation as everyone felt God's glory in the moment. Few had dry eyes that day.

Amid the praise, I leaned down to whisper to Alex, "This is not about you." He rolled his eyes at me—his favorite gesture, which has multiple meanings. In this case, I interpreted it as, "Daddy, that's what I've been telling you all along!" His trial and subsequent experiences had made him wise in the faith, even as a little guy. He said he had been to Heaven. People might question someone else saying such an outlandish thing, but in Alex's case, no one doubted it because it was all too clear that something had radically changed this six-year-old boy. Someone had brought him back to life when he seemed to be dying. Someone had healed his vertebrae. Someone had awakened his mind and awareness when we were told it was extremely unlikely. And Someone clearly had future plans for Alex Malarkey.

For Alex, it's all about that Someone. There has never been a moment when he took one iota of credit or reacted to a compliment in any way other than to redirect the glory to God. My greatest goal in life is to attain that mind-set myself, to become a billboard for Heaven rather than a sign of the times.

As the worship service progressed, the spirited songs of praise continued. Alex sang along with the congregation. I kept an eye on his face, because I love seeing him exalt God in music. Soon people began to stand and talk spontaneously about the amazing impact that their interaction with Alex had had on their lives. What a blessed day that was. Our hearts needed it so much.

Many months later at another service, where Alex was singing with the children's choir, my mind went back to the morning before the accident. Alex was so shy and clingy. In a way, this was a shy child's worst nightmare—every eye fixed on him. But Alex was a different creature now. He didn't want to be a spectacle, and we didn't want him to be one either. If he could have an ordinary experience of singing with the children's choir, it was a wonderful answer to the kind of prayer we had sent frantically to Heaven when he was in his coma. Having him back was the best we could have hoped for, and if by the grace of God he could have the normal experiences that other children enjoy—well, that was even better.

Not long afterward, there was yet another service—a special

Sunday evening gathering at our home. Here was another use of our "dream home" that we'd never dreamed of. Hundreds flooded in from all over central and western Ohio. After parking in our church lot, people boarded shuttle buses that brought them to our home. The church men struck again, setting up a sound system under a large oak tree, in an open area near the house. Pastors from different churches spoke. Then, once again, there was a time of sharing. We kept hearing about miracles, about good things happening in people's lives through God's showing His greatness in what the world saw as a tragedy.

Alex stayed off to the side and listened quietly on this particular evening. He was asked to speak, but he declined. After all, he said, this service wasn't in his honor—it was all about God. The right thing to do was to let God speak. My amazing son sat in the background, where he was most comfortable, and listened . . . as God did just that.

From Alex
Telling Others

Don't let anyone think less of you because you are young.
Be an example to all believers in what you say, in the
way you live, in your love, your faith, and your purity.

I TIMOTHY 4:12

My relationship with Jesus isn't different from anyone else's who knows Him; He just gave me a very special experience.

I want people to know that God is real and Heaven is real. God is my Daddy in Heaven, and He understands me all the time. That's how He feels about all His children.

Someday I want to be a missionary. I want to go different places where the gospel isn't clearly spoken and speak God into people and have God help me do that. I want people to understand that Heaven isn't a place where you go just because you do good things. You have to ask Jesus into your heart and ask for forgiveness.

If I'm not able to be a missionary, I want to be a catcher for the Houston Astros. Houston is a cool city. I could go to Texas games, plus it's warm there during the winters. And if I can't be a missionary or a baseball player, I want to be a comedian. I'm funny, and I have every joke book in the English language.

CHAPTER 8

WAR AND PEACE

"Hi, Daddy," Alex said weakly. "I'm being attacked."

TIME IS A quiet miracle worker, healing, bestowing wisdom, and providing perspective.

Time was doing its work, making routine that which was once traumatic. Hospital trips were no longer distressing. Alex struggled along, making great progress on some fronts. Beth cared for the children. I went back to work and began rebuilding my business. Our family gradually found its rhythm, and periodically we enjoyed rest along the way. But permanent peace in this life is not to be found. That's what the next world will look like, not this one. Spiritual warfare is occurring at all times. Isn't that why the Bible speaks of the necessity of spiritual armor? We may be oblivious to it, but that doesn't change the reality of Ephesians 6:12. There are forces at work that attempt to destroy everything God wants to do among us—and there is the "still, small voice" calling us to prayer, to vigilance, to standing against the enemy.

I wasn't thinking about any of that sitting in church on a warm Sunday morning in August 2005. In those days, I was confident our biggest battles were behind us. It was gratifying to know that things had calmed down—that most of the real surprises had already happened. Our life was reasonably normal, at least our kind of normal. Alex was back in the hospital with a lung infection, but the doctors told us it was manageable.

A smile down at Aaron reminded me that he was just a year younger than Alex had been when the accident occurred. Suddenly, an odd sensation pierced my mind. A thought burst into my consciousness, as clear as if Pastor Brown had spoken it from the pulpit: *Alex is going to be healed.* I tried to block it out, but like the phone that won't stop ringing until you answer it, I couldn't: *Alex is going to be healed.*

Alex being healed was hardly a new idea. I'd heard that earnest conviction from friends on countless occasions. "God is going to *completely* heal Alex," they would say. "I just know it's true. I can feel it!"

The first to say it, of course, had been Dave the paramedic, and then Beth herself, on the day of the accident. Many months of doctors, nurses, ambulances, mucous blockages, and ventilators hadn't dampened Beth's belief. She was certain the miracle was coming. Many of her friends had taken up the refrain. *God is going to heal Alex. It's coming, just believe it!*

I certainly *liked* that message and had no trouble accepting it, after a certain fashion. From the very beginning, God had been stretching our faith. It could be argued that His blessing Alex, taking him to

Heaven, sending ministering angels, and the rest were clearly part of a trend that would culminate in the grand finale of the full healing of our son—if you were given to that way of thinking. As a matter of fact, even if you didn't believe in God, you had to believe in Alex. His courage, determination, and tenacious spirit were the raw materials of a victory of mind over body. However, we did believe in God, and we knew that all things are possible in Christ.

I heard from God in my own way. I spent time with Him daily, studied His Word, and prayed constantly. But I wasn't one of those people who hear prophetic messages from God's lips to my ear . . . until that August day in church, sitting beside Aaron. That's when I finally got the memo.

One minute I was closely following the pastor's words, and the next I was hearing:

He will be fully healed.

I shrugged it off and went back to listening to the pastor, but it kept coming:

He will be fully healed.

The message was so persistent, I knew it wasn't coming from me. But I was not eager to embrace the idea of "hearing voices." It wasn't something I'd ever experienced. Could I accept, in faith, that this was God speaking? It was a huge commitment—the kind of commitment that will break your heart if fully yet falsely embraced. It was the kind of idea that convinces people you're out of your mind if you walk around telling everyone. It was okay for my wife and her friends, but I had a scientific mind-set, in keeping with my occupation. This just wasn't me.

But the Giver of that message was determined to hammer it home. Those five words took on a power of their own, assaulting the fortress of my intellect. It was time to come to terms with what so many had already embraced. God was ready for me to know that He was going to heal Alex. Was I ready to receive it?

Was I supposed to feel joy? I can't say I did. This development was too strange, too frightening. *Alex is going to be healed.* It was Beth's brand of faith, not the careful, analytical type I preferred. It was great for her, not for me. But suddenly, there I was, walking with her in the twilight zone of faith.

Is God bound by my intellectual understanding? What was keeping me from embracing a wonderful truth—fear, unbelief, pride? Then, in a moment, the mercy and greatness of God overwhelmed my tiny intellect, and He gave me the faith to believe. I simply *knew* God was speaking truth to me: *Alex is going to be healed.* I accepted the message, believed it, and received it, and when I did, a new message was impressed on my heart.

Go forward and pray.

God was literally instructing me to walk to the front of the sanctuary and ask for prayer. I touched Aaron's arm and whispered, "Would you come forward with me for prayer?"

He gave me a look and said, "No way, Daddy! They'll crush us."

I grinned. Aaron knew this church pretty well by now. They get very excited, very enthusiastic about the opportunity to pray with you. If you're a little boy, that stampede is a bit frightening.

God wanted prayer; Aaron wanted to avoid being squashed.

It seemed important for Aaron to be with me. I thought about it a minute. "Aaron," I whispered, "if you'll go up front for prayer with me, I'll take you to Dairy Queen after the service."

That offer (bribe!) proved too enticing to a young boy, even one confronted with being flattened by God's people. So we were all set when the pastor asked, "Would anyone like to approach the altar for prayer?" And up we stood.

Dave was one of the prayer leaders in our church. He would wait in the front of the sanctuary, greet those who came forward, and accompany them in lifting up their requests. As he took my hand, I told him, "God is going to heal Alex."

He replied, "I know he is," as if this were old news. "Is that what you want to pray about?"

I said, "He just told me."

We began talking to God, and people began flowing toward us and joining in. At some point there came a shout from about eight layers of people back. "Have you prayed against the devil?" Little did I know that this question would soon become key to Alex's life.

"I told you they'd crush us," said Aaron after it was over. But there was a big smile on his face.

I laughed. "Let's go. I owe you a trip to Dairy Queen."

As I stood at the counter, the man taking our order kept looking intently at us. It was becoming awkward, so finally I met his gaze with a curious demeanor.

"You don't remember me, do you?" he asked, the serious look remaining on his face.

I hate it when people say that. Smiling politely, I only proved him correct. He kept on with the guessing game, which of course makes things even more uncomfortable.

"Come on. You're sure my face doesn't ring a bell?"

"I'm sorry; we've had a lot going on. You're going to have to help me out."

He said, "My name is Chris. I was at the accident scene, next to your car . . . with your son. I prayed for him to be all right."

"That's incredible! You were there?"

"Yes, I was."

I looked at him, amazed at the greatness of God. Dairy Queen on Sunday was not a planned stop. Without the direction of God, I might never have met Chris. From a human perspective, life is random, and sometimes random turns out well. But I know God put Chris directly in my path that Sunday.

+++ The accident is something I don't think about often. It's just not something you experience every day—being with someone when you think he's passed away.

The Sunday morning of the accident, my family and I were working in our front yard. All of a sudden we heard brakes skidding and a sound I'll never forget. I told the girls to call 911 and took off running toward the accident. When I got in the backseat with Alex, his head was hanging down and he couldn't get air. I desperately wanted to help him, but I knew enough not to touch him. I just kept talking to Alex and telling him to hang on, help was coming. And then I saw him take his last breath. I watched his body shudder and almost relax, if that's the right word.

I walked away from that scene believing that Alex had died. I went back to my wife and kids and said, "We need to pray for this family and that boy because in a couple of days I think we're going to read his name in the paper." From what I saw, I just felt he was passing . . . he was going to Heaven.

Chris Leasure, eyewitness to the accident
who got into the car with Alex before Dan Tullis arrived +++

Chris looked down at Aaron, with eyes a little wet. "Is . . . is this him?"

"No," I said gently. "This is his younger brother Aaron. Alex is in the hospital with an infection in his lungs. But he's doing better." I reached out and took his hand. "He's doing better because people like you have been there to pray for him. Thank you, Chris. Thanks for praying that day. God answered you."

God never seems to be quite finished astounding us with wonder and amazement.

Defense

After spending a little time at home that afternoon, I headed to the hospital. Alex and I would spend the night together. The events of that day played over in my mind: God's telling me that Alex would be healed; being directed to seek the church's prayer; the surge of power and faith I felt as everyone laid hands on us and lifted us before the throne of God; then, in the wake of that prayer experience, immediately crossing paths with a key prayer warrior from the beginning of the journey. What an amazing day! I couldn't wait to tell Alex all about it.

My spirits were high as I rounded the corner with a smile and entered Alex's room. The moment I saw him, however, my spirit froze. Alex seemed desperate to see me. I'd never seen him like this.

"How's my boy?" I asked, searching his worried face.

"Hi, Daddy," Alex said weakly. "I'm being attacked."

The smile vanished from my face.

"What?" I asked. "What do you mean, Son?"

Alex looked pale, drained, frightened. "The devil—he's attacking me. He's saying terrible things. I want to make him go away."

I felt a knot form in the pit of my stomach. Alex had never said anything like this before.

"Oh, Alex, Daddy is right here. And God is with us too. Everything is going to be all right."

Trembling, teary, and clearly in pain, Alex looked into my eyes and said, "I can't say His name, Daddy."

"Whose name, Alex?"

My mind raced to understand what he could mean. He had already said the devil's name. And then it dawned on me.

"Jesus? You're having trouble saying the name of Jesus?"

With frantic eyes, Alex said yes. A sense of panic rose in my chest. This was new territory for me. I wanted to help. I'd do anything and everything to help my son, but I didn't know what to do.

"Alex," I said, "would you like to pray with someone special? What about Jay?"

Jay was a friend of ours, a man of prayer, and a man of wisdom on spiritual matters. He really knew how to pray.

"Yes, Daddy, call Jay."

Jay was quick to pick up the line.

"Jay, it's Kevin. Listen, I've got a situation with Alex. He's being attacked by the devil, and he can't call out to Jesus. Would you pray with him?"

"Of course, let's pray."

I held the phone to Alex's ear, and in moments an amazing transformation took place before my eyes. The tension slowly loosened and melted away. The color gradually seeped into his cheeks. The fright in his eyes mostly melted away. As I thanked Jay and hung up the phone, Alex smiled. He looked at me and said, "I can say His name now. *Jesus. Jesus. Jesus!*"

I laughed, held his hand, and we said Jesus' name together several times. No name has ever sounded more beautiful. We relaxed, joked around, and made small talk for fifteen minutes, but then things took another ominous turn. The fright had returned to Alex's eyes.

"Alex, are you all right? Is it the same thing as before?"

He signaled yes.

"Do you want Daddy to call Jay again?"

"No, Daddy. I want just us to do it."

"Well, then, that's what we'll do, Alex. Let's you and me start praying, okay?"

For about an hour, the two of us petitioned God, talked quietly together for an interval, prayed a bit more, then talked some more. By a quarter after ten that night, Alex was all right again, and we slept peacefully together at the hospital.

The following morning, the phone began to ring.

"Hello, Kevin, this is Jay. I have a question. Was there another satanic attack against Alex?"

"As a matter of fact, yes," I said. "How did you know?"

He said, "Did it end at 10:15?"

"That's exactly when it was over," I answered. "Tell me what's going on. How did you know all this?"

"After Alex and I prayed over the phone," he said, "I felt that I needed to keep praying. I was down on the floor, on my face, talking

+++

Alex asked me if I was mad at him for being tempted by Satan, and I told him that the devil only messes with people who are a threat to him. Alex is one giant threat to the evil one, and we need to continually pray for him.

PrayforAlex.com
post by Kevin Malarkey
on August 9, 2005

to the Lord. I was lifting up Alex and praying against Satan for at least an hour. In my spirit, I looked up and saw the feet of God before me. I looked up farther and saw that God was seated on the throne, holding a scepter. Then I heard His voice say, 'It is finished.' At that point I stopped praying and went to bed. It was 10:15."

Later I thought through all the events of that day, from church in the morning to the intensity of the spiritual warfare I encountered in my son's hospital room. What if I had ignored that still, small voice telling me that Alex would be healed and that I should go to the altar and call the church to pray on this matter? What if our friend Mary Lou hadn't suggested we pray against Satan? As a result, we had the power of the church's prayer working for us when the satanic attack came. When Jay, Alex, and I all prayed for that hour, God finally said, "It is finished." And it was—for that day, anyway.

What if I had just slept late that day? What if any of us had simply ignored the urgings inside us? What if our minds had been elsewhere or we had refused to acknowledge what was clearly God's voice? Would it have gone worse for my son? I don't know the answer to this question, but that day persuaded me how important it is to listen and obey when God calls.

Going Off Road

Even when we arrived home, our needs were lovingly met, day by day, and there's no better example than the way they helped us strengthen our "fortress"—our home base.

Getting Alex in or out of the house was problematic. There were four steps to the front door and three to the garage. Moving Alex about, as light as he was, involved lifting both him and his chair about three feet off the ground.

A ramp was the obvious solution, but we couldn't figure out where to put it or how to design it in accordance with our home's layout. We were also a little uncomfortable with giving in to a permanently installed ramp—it felt like surrender, a resignation that God would never heal Alex. We said okay to the ramp, but we called it a "bike ramp." After all, there was no doubt that our kids would use it that way.

That's where our friend Wayne came in.

Wayne had a creative vision. He figured out an angle from the house to the driveway, just to the left of a large tree. For safe use with the wheelchair, the ramp would have to decline one inch per foot. The total drop, we knew, would come out to thirty-nine inches. When we measured, the length of Wayne's proposed ramp was *exactly* thirty-nine feet—just as if God had intervened in the original building of our house thirty years ago to make a perfect place for it. I think He probably did.

Alex could get in and out now without the heavy lifting. The next thing we needed was to be able to get him down to the lower level of our house. The problem was that our only access to that floor was by a spiral staircase. Since we have a walkout basement, it made sense to build a sidewalk that would connect to the ramp at the driveway.

We were able to have some fun with the sidewalk, because there are few limitations in how you can build it in a rural setting. We scrawled our kids' names and the date in the wet cement. Then, as a final touch, Beth wrote, "With God all things are possible."

We believe that, by the way. We believe that one day Alex will step right over that verse as he walks along the pavement.

Yet the problems continued. A friend of ours checked the plumbing and was appalled by what he found. The pipes were a mess, and there was no water filtration system. He wouldn't fix the plumbing without a water-conditioning system, which would cost about five thousand dollars.

I sighed heavily at the thought of another huge expense. Apparently I hadn't learned my lesson. The friend shoved a piece of paper into my hand. "Here, call this number and pick out the system you want," he said. "Don't worry about the price."

"What do you mean?" I asked.

"Well, I've prayed about this thing," he said. "I feel that God is asking for my credit card on this expenditure. The full amount." He expressed his confidence that God would supply the money by the time the credit card bill came due.

It was another beautiful gift, one that was entirely essential to our needs due to the decrepit condition of the plumbing in the house.

We met with the company and chose the most basic model. Our friend, however, would not accept that. He upgraded the order to the more expensive model, one with extra features. He was confident about what God wanted him to do. And sure enough, it turned out that a customer returned the exact model two days after purchase, unused, and we received the returned unit at a huge discount.

A few weeks later, I was sitting in a church service. Two of the three morning announcements concerned Alex. The first of these was a simple update on his progress and a request for people to keep praying for our family and ministering to us. The second was an in-depth story about our plumbing. It's humbling to hear every challenge of your family life shared before a congregation. One of the best proofs of God's existence is the love we see among His people.

The speaker said, "As you know, the Malarkeys are having a system installed for softening the water. A Columbus friend put $4,200 on his credit card and trusted God for the funding within thirty days. This past Friday the bill came due, and on Monday we had only collected $1,300. We didn't announce this, but simply trusted God to supply the need.

"On Friday, the total we had collected was $5,200. The company was paid in full, and as for the balance—Kevin, if you're present today, please see the pastor after the service. He has a check for your family in the amount of $1,000."

Naturally, that money was another gift from God, used to pay bills and buy equipment that Alex needed. We also were finally able to get a power wheelchair that would allow Alex to drive himself around using a control he operated with his chin. Once we were able to get it, Alex gained a sense of autonomy in moving around without having to be dependent upon others. If he wanted to go to the next room, he could do it. If he wanted to move to the end of our driveway, he could.

As long as we were all careful, this new freedom was a wonderful thing for Alex.

Let's Roll!

God met every one of our needs and so much more. One of the most basic needs, transportation for our family, however, continued to be a juggling act. The pattern of our family life and our unique challenges made going to church difficult, at best. As much as we desired to be able to go places as a family, we simply couldn't.

When another Easter Sunday came and we were unable to go to church as a family, I was very discouraged. Easter is my favorite day on the calendar, but we had no way to transport Alex to church. His power wheelchair, great as it is, requires a van with sufficient space and special equipment to secure it while driving.

As I sat at home on Easter feeling unhappy, the phone rang. Beth picked it up and I heard her say, "Hi, Suzanne."

Suzanne, a speech therapist, had done a swallow test for Alex several months earlier. At that point, it had been a year since Alex had eaten on his own. The doctors had told us he would never be able to do so again, due to his inability to swallow. So this was another goal, another area for God to speak in and to drown out the doctors' declarations of the impossible.

Alex, Beth, and I made an elaborate list of the first fifty things Alex would eat when he could, the first of them being Mr. Sullivan's gravy. He was a friend who had made a dish for us with wonderful gravy. I put a dab of it on Alex's tongue and then wiped it away. It was a swallow test, one he passed, and it made Suzanne a hero in our family.

As Beth continued to speak with Suzanne, tears began to flow down her cheeks. What was going on? Beth was crying about a swallow test? After Beth hung up, she explained.

Suzanne had told her pastor at Christ Our King Church, Robin Ricks, that she knew a family who needed a van. That very morning, before the Easter service started, Pastor Ricks had stood on the platform and said, "Friends, the Lord spoke to me this morning while I was praying. Would you like to hear what He has laid upon my heart? It's about a little boy whom I've never met. His name is Alex Malarkey, and he was severely injured in an automobile accident. This boy loves the Lord, but he can't go to church without the kind of van that will accommodate his wheelchair. He has other places he needs to go too.

"As I prayed this morning, I saw a picture in my mind of Alex looking out the window of a van, on his way to worship God. I also felt a strong impression that, even though I drove here this morning, I would not look out the windshield of my own car again until I promised to see that the money is raised for that little boy and his family to have a van. It's very clear to me what God wants us to do this morning as an act of obedience. Let's buy that family the van it needs."

He explained that this special collection would not preempt the church's regular offering—that would be at the normal time, and folks would give their tithes and offerings as usual. Donations for Alex would be separate. The giving for the van started, and within five minutes, a group of fewer than four hundred people had raised eighteen thousand dollars. Not a single one of them had met Alex . . . as far as I knew.

Examples of sacrificial giving were everywhere in evidence that day. One young man, fifteen-year-old Eric, had been working for friends of his parents but hadn't yet received his wages. After hearing what Pastor Ricks said, he found the woman he had worked for in the lobby of the church and asked her to write the check, making the entire amount payable to the van fund. There were many other stories of giving from the heart. When that money arrived, we were absolutely stunned, and we're still thanking God.

+++

I often tell others about how Christ Our King Church raised the money for a van in less than thirty minutes on Easter Sunday. They did not even know the boy or realize that the accident had occurred right in front of their church.

Dr. William Malarkey,
Kevin's father

Reenlisting

It was fun to look out the window and see the new van parked in our driveway. What an amazing gift from God, through His people. Beth and I were eager to meet the pastor who had said he had heard from God on our behalf. Accepting our invitation for a visit, he came to the house. Over the course of getting to know each other, I asked a typical question: "Where's your church located?"

"It's at the intersection of Route 47 and Route 9."

My heart skipped a beat. "That's where the accident was, Pastor."

His eyes were large. Maybe he thought this was an awkward development, something that might bring us pain. But it wasn't, of course. We don't curse that location, but see it as a place where God's destiny took an amazing turn in our lives—one filled with pain and uphill struggles, but one destined to glorify His name and ultimately bless our family.

+++ When I first met Alex, I realized that he was a young kid who had a strong sense of who God is. It was really evident that his faith was strong. I never remember feeling bad for him. As I was communicating with Alex, I could just sense the presence of God with him in his smiles, in his questions—and, boy, did he have a lot of questions.

Pastor Robin Ricks, Christ Our King Church +++

Pastor Ricks spoke to Alex for some time, and the two of them hit it off. I was fascinated, and (to be honest) just a little bit awed by the way the two of them talked about the unseen world—the realm of angels and demons and spiritual warfare. It was clear that these two were kindred spirits, who had both notched some experience in that world.

We felt an amazing bond with this man. Before he left, he asked if he could pray with us. That's the normal way to finish a pastoral visit. But there was nothing normal about this prayer. Pastor Ricks spoke to God with an incredible intimacy, reflecting the relationship he clearly had with the Lord. His words reflected authority and humility at the same time. It was one of the most amazing moments of spiritual communion with God that I've ever experienced.

We were delighted to have a new friend in Christ, especially someone who could stand beside us in the trenches of spiritual warfare. We didn't see Pastor Ricks again until two years later, when we visited Christ Our King Church for a Saturday afternoon children's activity. The moment we walked into the church, we felt the presence of God's Spirit in a palpable way. Immediately we wanted to be a part of it, and before we left that afternoon, I looked at Beth and said, "Are we going to . . . ?"

"Yes!" she said quickly, with a big smile.

The next morning we attended worship at Christ Our King Church and have been regular attendees ever since. We've stayed close to our "old" church family—those wonderful folks will be our friends for life—but God was moving us onward, reenlisting us in a new unit, if you will. Over time, God puts us in different settings with different groups of people. I think the dynamic of Christ Our King Church was exactly what He knew would minister to us at this point in our lives, when we had so many needs. And of course, we hope we can minister to these people in return.

+++

In 2008, near Christmas, a team from Christ Our King Church came over to install new flooring in Alex's bedroom. Sometime during the day, one of the workers approached me and said, "You don't know me, but we go way back . . . about four years."

My mind raced a little trying to place him.

"Have we met before?"

He held out his hand. "Dan Tullis," he said as he shook mine and nodded. "Well, yes, but you might not remember. It was on the day of your accident. We hadn't been home from church that long when we heard this deafening crash. I ran to the intersection, just a couple hundred feet from our house. When I got there, I climbed into the backseat with Alex. I prayed over him and tried to comfort him, even though I didn't know if he was alive. I stayed there until the paramedics arrived. He wasn't breathing, that I could tell."

"And here you are, four years later, working on my house and telling me this. And did you say that you were a member of Christ Our King at the time?"

"Yes. When our church family helped buy the van, I had no idea who it went to until you came to church a couple of years later."

"So we've been going to the same church for a while now, but you never approached me with this story?"

"This just seemed like the right time, I guess!"

"Dan, thank you so much for your ministry to Alex."

"You bet, brother."

I had now met two people sent by God to the scene of the accident to pray for Alex in the most amazing, "serendipitous" ways. I serve an awesome God!

Heavenly Languages

When it's time for him to sleep, we often place a sheet over Alex's face. He likes to sleep in total darkness. One evening after Alex had been asleep for quite a while, strange noises came from under the sheet. Looking up from what I was reading, I laughed. Was this Alex's way of saying, "Could you open the curtain for me, please?" Pulling the sheet back, I was surprised to see that Alex was still sleeping, yet the unfamiliar sounds continued. Was this some new way of snoring? I began to listen closer. There was a pattern, a cadence to the sounds he was making, like a garbled dream or mumblings from another language.

He was in no discernible stress, so I didn't wake him. The murmurings continued. About ten minutes later Alex opened his eyes wide.

"Daddy, I was just talking to God in Heaven."

"Were you really, Alex?" I asked. "That's pretty cool, because we could hear you speaking—it sounded strange!"

"You could hear me?" he asked with surprise.

"Yes. It sounded like words from a language I don't know."

A few minutes later, he drifted off to sleep again, and the strange sounds resumed. Aaron, who was seven, walked into the room. One look at Alex and he began laughing. Then he realized that Alex was asleep.

Alex was awake again a few minutes later with Aaron sitting next to him.

"What were you doing?" Aaron asked, a little unsure.

"I was talking to God in Heaven," he said. "It's in another language."

Not long ago, Alex made another surprise announcement: "There's a spirit here, in the bedroom, but I can't tell what kind of spirit it is."

Since his otherworldly experiences had begun, Alex had always known an angel from a demon. But this time was different.

"Well, what does it look like?" I asked.

"Like you," he answered.

This caught me off guard, so I laughed. "Got to be an angel, then," I said, smiling.

But Alex wasn't laughing. His brow was wrinkled.

"Why don't you use your Heaven language and ask?" Aaron suggested.

Alex thought for a moment, then turned to Aaron and said, "Do you promise not to laugh?"

Aaron gave a very solemn promise. I shook my head in wonder at this conversation between a nine- and an eleven-year-old.

"Would you cover my face?" Alex asked.

Soon after Aaron placed the sheet back over his face, the language from Alex's earlier sleeping experience was audible once again. He continued speaking in his "Heaven language," as Aaron had called it, and then he fell silent. After a moment, Alex's normal voice asked us to pull back the sheet.

"It was an angel," Alex said. "He came here to comfort me. He touched my head."

Ongoing Angels

We've had these little adventures from time to time, but the presence of angels has been a consistent reality. From the time of the accident, Alex says, the angels have graced our home. Up to the time he was about eight—the period of Alex's most serious physical struggle—there was a particular group of angels that would surround his bed in our master bedroom.

Alex knew them all by name, and he would carry on conversations with them. John, Vent, and Ryan were names he mentioned. A typical reaction, of course, is to observe that a little boy on a ventilator, who has a baby brother named Ryan, is going to give those names to his imaginary friends. We know that children create imaginary friends to help them cope with new and difficult situations. Passing tedious hours in a wheelchair without the use of anything below his neck would surely inspire a child's imagination as a coping mechanism. Couldn't this explain these bizarre angel adventures, as well as the suspiciously familiar names? I wrestled with these doubts for a long time.

In the end, if what we see, hear, or read strains credibility, we must choose whether to believe it. It's not my job to convince you. But in fairness, I'll make this point about the veracity of Alex's claims. Just as when you see a tree swaying mightily in the wind, you know there is a powerful force behind the movement, so the look that comes across Alex's face when he sees angels reveals that he is in powerful yet unseen company.

Margaret, our friend who was in the hospital room when we first became aware of Alex's heavenly visitors, wrote the following words on our Web site after that first amazing experience: "I wish everyone reading these words could see Alex's face. He was truly radiant!"

Radiant, like the face of Stephen, whose face was as bright as an angel's when the Holy Spirit came over him (Acts 6:15). The paths of many people have crossed our own during these months and years—as many as one hundred people have been present during the kinds of experiences I've described. I haven't met a single one who has doubted that Alex was speaking the truth or suspected that he was delusional.

One day when our friend Laryn was at our house playing checkers, I asked, "Laryn, you've heard Alex describe his visits to the heavenly realm. What is your honest opinion . . . about what Alex reports?"

"Kevin, I have no earthly idea what that boy is talking about. But the deepest place in my heart that is aware of God *screams* when Alex's lips move."

That's quite a statement, but I know precisely what he's talking about: Alex's experience has an infectious component to it. You *feel* what he's talking about.

It's hard to say, "You had to be there" and to expect that to suffice. I can only hope God's Spirit communicates through our words in this book so that you can picture yourself in the room with my son.

We've come to believe there are angels around our family at all times. The Bible hints at "guardian angels." For example, we read, "For he will order his angels to protect you wherever you go" (Psalm 91:11). And Jesus once said about children, "Beware that you don't look down on any of these little ones. For I tell you that in heaven their angels are always in the presence of my heavenly Father" (Matthew 18:10). An angel protected Daniel from the lions (Daniel 6:21-22), and when Peter was miraculously released from prison, his friends heard his voice at the door and said, "It must be his angel" (Acts 12:15). It's clear in the Bible that angels often minister, serve, and protect people, but we can't be certain whether there is a lifelong guardian angel for every believer.

We observed a pattern in the ministry of angels to our family.

When Alex's life is calm, the angels are silent and discreet, if not altogether absent; when Alex struggles, their activity increases. During his first year home, when we went back and forth to the hospital so often, there was almost daily talk of angels. That pattern actually undermines the idea that angels are the figment of a bored child's imagination—our angels arrive with the problems and excitement. Every single time Alex was in the hospital, I heard about them. When he is at home and doing well, weeks may pass with no mention of them.

I know that we have more courage and less anxiety when we feel the assurance that angels are watching over us. We feel strong in the Lord.

But there are other visitors, too—and those aren't as friendly.

From Alex

Demons

We are not fighting against flesh-and-blood enemies,
but against evil rulers and authorities of the unseen
world, against mighty powers in this dark world,
and against evil spirits in the heavenly places.

EPHESIANS 6:12

One day I wanted to tell my daddy something important. I told him that he had to promise me he wouldn't be sad. This is not a sad thing, but a happy thing, I said.

After he said okay, I told him that there are two days I look forward to more than any others in my life.

The first is the day I die. You see, I really can't wait to get home. It's not that I want to die right now; I'm not sad.

It's not that I'm sick of all this and want to leave. It's just that Heaven is my home. I want to go back to it.

The second is the day when the devil goes to the lake of fire. I can't wait for him to be gone for good.

I remember the devil telling me a lie in the car accident: "Your daddy is dead, and it's your fault!" He is the father of lies, and I am so glad I know now that he is a liar.

Sometimes I have visitors I don't want to have—my daddy knows the sound of my voice when this is happening, and he comes to pray with me.

But I don't always need him to come, since he taught me how to pray. The demons leave when they hear the name of Jesus. Daddy told me about what Jesus taught his followers: "I have given you authority over all the power of the enemy" (Luke 10:19).

So I say, "Devil—or demons—in Jesus' name, leave my room and leave this house. By the blood of Jesus, I command you to go. Leave me alone."

Once my brother Aaron ended my prayer with, "Bye-bye, Snake Boy!"

Sometimes my daddy doesn't know if the evil spirits have left the room—but I always know! There is peace again.

My daddy asks me what it is like to be around a demon. Well, it's evil, scary, and ugly! They accuse me of things, bring me doubt, make me feel sad, and tell me I will never be healed and that God won't protect me.

I know these things sound bad, but I also know something much better: "The Spirit who lives in [us] is greater than the spirit who lives in the world" (1 John 4:4). My God is true and faithful and loving. He's perfect!

Everyone is curious about the devil, what he looks like. I don't want to talk about this! The devil is scary! But I can tell you a few things.

The devil is the ugliest thing imaginable. He has three heads. All the heads are the same and have hair on top made of fire. He's got beaming red eyes with flames for pupils, and his nose is nasty and torn up. Each of the heads speaks different lies at the same time. He speaks to me in English, but his voice is screechy like a witch and changes into different sounds.

The devil's mouth is funny looking, with only a few moldy teeth. And I've never noticed any ears.

His body has a human form, with two bony arms and two bony legs. He has no flesh on his body, only some moldy stuff. His robes are torn and dirty.

I don't know about the color of the skin or robes—it's all just too scary to concentrate on these things!

My daddy asked me if the devil takes on different forms when I see him. No. He is always the same freaky devil.

The devil usually comes alone. Sometimes I can see him, but usually I just feel him—that's more than enough! It's hard to find the right words for all of this—the devil is truly indescribable.

Demons are often green. They have hair made of fire, and

their skin and robes are just like the devil's, too. The eyes are the same, and demons have long fingernails. Sometimes they're alone, but they're more likely than the devil to attack in groups.

I don't count them or look too closely because it's so scary. When it's angels, I know them and their names, but one demon is just like another to me.

What do they do? They walk around telling people lies.

There's a spiritual war that never stops—angels against demons.

CHAPTER 9

ENDINGS AND BEGINNINGS

I wish you could see his eyes, hear his voice, and sense the fragrance of Heaven about this young and innocent boy, all wrapped up in a few simple words that he shares, and the manner in which he shares them.

THE BOY WHO came back from Heaven was the son we knew, but something more. He had been "away from [his] earthly bod[y] . . . [and] at home with the Lord" (2 Corinthians 5:8), and the experience had changed him forever. It took us some time to understand that.

When Alex emerged from his coma in January 2005, he rejoined our world gradually. It was like seeing someone slowly push out of a fog separating two different realities. He was present without being fully aware. Like a newborn baby, he had to learn how to make sense of this world.

As the days went by, Alex's mind began interpreting the information from his senses. His conscious mind was going back to work. He quickly learned how to communicate, using rudimentary signs for yes and no. Soon he was capable of forming words with his mouth, giving him access to a world of more complex ideas and expressions.

Even at this point, as basic as his messages were, he was signaling to us that he had been to places and seen things that we couldn't imagine. Yet so much was still beyond his ability to explain.

From our perspective, our son had been a sleeping six-year-old boy in a hospital bed. Our prayers were focused simply on bringing him back, on seeing his eyes open, and on being able to tell him we loved him. Then, knowing we serve a loving God, we dared to hope that the Alex we had raised from infancy, our unique and recognizable Alex, would return to us.

Dwelling in the invisible world had sharpened Alex's spiritual senses far beyond what is ordinary for a little boy. It left him with a powerful longing to be with his Lord and Savior once again, whether in the flesh or in the spirit. It even endowed him with a new sense of humor that was the substance of inner joy.

Even before Alex emerged from the coma, people would come out of his room after prayer and tell us they had experienced something spiritually powerful, just from speaking to God beside his bed. Today many more are being transformed by Alex and his life. He has opened up just a little bit about what he saw and learned, though there are aspects of it he still won't discuss—in some cases, details about Heaven that he has been told not to share.

In late 2006 and into 2007, Alex began to tell us more about angels, demons, and Heaven itself. We already had a basic understanding of his experience—his trip to Heaven, his encounter with spiritual beings, and so on. We knew he'd had what is commonly called a near-death experience, and we realized he wasn't the first person to come back with such an account. It was true that he had spoken of seeing angels during the time he was emerging from his coma. And we knew miracles had already occurred: the vertebrae

+++ I've been amazed by Alex's closeness to Jesus. One day his dad, Kevin, had a question for me:

"Jami, I don't want this to come out wrong, but . . . well . . . I'm starting to wonder if Alex has something of a prophetic gift. I know it sounds a little funny, but—"

"Prophetic gift," I interrupted, "you don't have to tell me. Two years ago, after church I was in the foyer pulling on my coat. I saw Alex in his wheelchair across the foyer and decided to go say hi. We talked for a little bit, and then just as I turned to leave, Alex said, 'Jami, you need to go home and read Deuteronomy 18.'

"'Okay, Alex, I'll do it. Can you tell me why I need to read Deuteronomy 18?'

"'God told me to tell you your son is coming home.'

"I just stared at him, Kevin. How did he know anything about my teenage prodigal son, living in a different city with his father? I had wanted him to come home so much and had been praying for him constantly. With the child support all arranged, it was out of the question, not to mention that he *wanted* to live with his father. But there Alex was, telling me my son was coming home. It was a bit of a shock to hear, but on the other hand, Alex says a lot of surprising things. I said good-bye and hurried home, sat down in a chair, and opened the Bible to Deuteronomy 18. The first verse talks about the establishment of the Levitical priesthood in the nation of Israel through the tribe of Levi. It took my breath away. Levi is the name of my prodigal teenage son. Two weeks later, my Levi moved back to live with me."

Jami Kreutzer, a family friend from church +++

in his neck had returned to their normal position without medical intervention, for one thing.

At that point, however, what we knew about the whole matter was only the tip of a vast, astonishing iceberg. As Alex regained the ability to communicate with more than labored, one-syllable words, he could tell us far more. For instance, Heaven is not the "next" world; it is *now*. Heaven is not in "the heavens" or the sky. It is everywhere and nowhere. Alex says it's hard to explain.

Our earthly minds struggle to understand a "place" that is not a place and a "time" with no past, present, or future, but only the eternal now. The earth, the sky, the cosmos, and time—these are things that God made. They are the home He made for us, and He enters into them to interact with us, but He doesn't live in space or time. Time will end, and even this universe will end. But God, His angels, and all of us who accept His gift will live together forever in Heaven.

Yet we didn't view these events as particularly unusual. For us, the time itself was unusual. Watching our son sleep for seven weeks—that was unusual. Our everyday lives had been turned upside down, and in a way, there *was* no usual—not for us. When life careens off course, we tend to expect the unexpected. So what was happening around Alex was probably less surprising to us than it may seem to you.

The years following Alex's return to our home, then, were about endings and beginnings—it was the end of Alex's coma and our dependence on the hospital. But it was also the beginning to a new and challenging kind of family life. Even more than this, it felt like the beginning of our awareness of another world, the powerful reality that continues to permeate our son's life.

I'm Not Allowed to Tell You

"I'm not allowed to tell you." I guess that I've heard that phrase several hundred times during the past five years. You see, I tend to pester Alex with a lot of questions. Who wouldn't? When someone in your household professes to visit Heaven, to see angels, and to watch demons flee, it piques your interest. But Alex doesn't appreciate questions that are asked merely to satisfy a curiosity rather than to draw near to God. I'm always intrigued by the kinds of questions Alex will answer and the kinds he won't. The details he gives are often surprising and unpredictable—the devil's having three heads when manifesting directly to Alex, for example, or angels' wings that look like "masks." Such things don't come from picture books, movies, or video games.

Alex knows where his boundaries lie, which subjects he is not to reveal. But there are other reasons he chooses not to speak. Alex often says, "Daddy, this isn't about me."

Alex truly doesn't want to make a big deal out of what he has seen. I think that when he first began sharing, he had no idea what the impact would be beyond his mommy and daddy. He is a shy boy, and what seemed to him like a pebble tossed into a lake created ripples that fanned out further than he could have ever expected. He's not crazy about the attention.

He's also well aware that others cannot see what he sees, and I know he wishes they could. I suppose it feels strange for him to know he has the only eyes that see certain realities. It has been said that in the land of the blind, the one-eyed man is king. Alex definitely has a sight most of us do not, but there is nothing in Alex that enjoys being "king."

When I try to talk to Alex about heavenly things, he is almost always uncomfortable. Some items he isn't permitted to discuss; other times he struggles to find the needed vocabulary. It can be difficult for him to determine what falls into those limited areas and what he can reveal.

Another reason Alex is sometimes reluctant to share all he has seen in Heaven is that he feels as if he's telling everyone, if you will, what's under the gift-wrapping of their Christmas presents. Alex has seen Christmas morning. He's had a sneak peek at wonderful, shining gifts marked "Do not open before Christmas" for the rest of us. He doesn't want to spoil the great joy we will all experience when we ourselves arrive in Heaven and toss away the ribbons and wrappings.

Thinking about that point, I asked, "What about you, Alex? Will your current experience of Heaven take anything away from the day when you go there forever?"

A massive smile came across his face. "No way. I can't wait to go!" That wonderful day pulls upon his heart with an irresistible spiritual magnetism. I then pointed out to him that if Heaven is too wonderful to be spoiled for him, the same could be true for the rest of us. So why not tell *us* what's inside a couple of those packages before Christmas?

He got the point and became slightly more generous with his details. But some matters remain off the record; his lips are sealed this side of eternity.

One day, as we talked over all these chapters, Alex said, "Daddy, are you sure we should really write this book?"

"Well, I did pray about it, Alex," I said. "But if you're uncomfortable with it, and if God doesn't give you a clear go-ahead, then we won't publish it. Can you tell me what you're struggling with?"

"I don't want people making a big deal about me."

"Well, I agree with that, and you know, no matter what we do or say, some people are probably going to do that anyway. What we have to share, though, is encouraging others. We want to help them think about God in new ways, and we want to bring honor and glory to His name. Even if some people make a big deal over you, won't it be worth it if many, many more of them make a big deal over Jesus?"

Alex remained quiet, betraying a continuing sense of unease.

"Alex," I began, attempting to help him see a broader picture, "some people in the Bible saw Heaven too. Take John, for instance. He traveled to Heaven and saw amazing things that he came back and wrote about for millions and millions of people to read. People are encouraged when they read about Heaven because they get a glimpse of the awesome majesty of God and are reminded that Heaven is a real place. In Revelation 4, John tells about how he saw angels with six wings—"

"I saw that!" Alex grinned.

I asked him to tell me more . . . and you have now heard his testimony in this book. We hope it brings the majesty of God alive for you in new ways so that your life can continue to grow in discipleship to Christ.

Alex is always delighted to discover that what he has seen is also described in the Bible. Naturally, Beth and I know exactly what Alex has and hasn't learned about the Bible, since we're the ones who have taught him from birth. And Alex has described countless details about Heaven that we know he had not previously learned from the Bible. For example, we never taught him the book of Revelation. We spent our time with Alex in the Gospel of John.

"Daddy, I'm just a kid!" Alex says. "I don't know all the stuff that's in the Bible. I just know what Jesus shows me."

Alex's Trips to Heaven Continue

Perhaps by now it is clear that Alex has been to Heaven several times, but the first trip on the day of the accident was different from what occurs now. At the time of the accident, Alex proceeded through a tunnel of light and had a series of interactions with angels and with God. At that time, he could also observe earthly events such as what happened at the accident site (even after the MedFlight chopper had already taken his body from the scene) and the emergency room, where he and Jesus watched as doctors operated on Alex's own body. He remembers the discussions concerning whether he would stay in Heaven or return to earth. Many of these reports seem fantastical, but they are not unprecedented in the realm of near-death/life-after-death experiences. Others who have gone to Heaven have described many details similar to Alex's experiences.

Alex's experiences have one major difference, however: he still periodically goes to Heaven. When does this happen? Mostly in his sleep. It also happens occasionally when he lies in bed awake. There's a certain regularity about how the visits progress. He arrives just inside the gates. He talks with the angels who stand guard. Those angels are usually buzzing with excitement about the day when Jesus will return to earth. And as usual, they always tell Alex not to be afraid.

"Alex, why do the angels always tell you not to be afraid? What do you think they are referring to?"

"I think the angels are talking about the glory of God."

This answer is consistent with Scripture. These powerful angels know they are talking to a human being, who is unaccustomed to the magnificence and unfiltered glory of God—what the Bible calls the *shekinah*. The Lord once granted Moses his request to see the awesome glory of God. But God told Moses to stand in a cleft of the rock as His glory passed by, and God protected him with His hand. Moses couldn't look upon the face of God and live. When Moses came down Mount Sinai to rejoin his people, Moses' face was glowing with God's reflected glory, and the Bible tells us that when the Israelites "saw the radiance of Moses' face, they were afraid to come near him" (Exodus 34:30).

Or consider those shepherds keeping watch over their flocks by night when Jesus was born. "An angel of the Lord appeared among them, and the radiance of the Lord's glory surrounded them. They were terrified" (Luke 2:9). There are many angelic visits recorded in Scripture where people were frightened at the sight of angels. No

---

+++ God knows how to extend grace to sustain a person. He has a way of bringing out glory from every situation, so I don't think it's so far-reaching that a loving God, a graceful Lord Jesus Christ, would touch a young man's life and show him things.

At the same time, we believe that the Bible is infallible. The Word of God is the final statement, and all things must be filtered through it. So if Alex says he's seen Heaven, we have to go through Scripture and ask, "Has anyone else seen Heaven?" And if that answer is yes, and since Jesus is the same yesterday, today, and forever, then it can be yes today. And that's the basis from which we evaluate all revelation— whether we're skeptical or whether we're believing—we evaluate all revelation from the Word of God. If God has done it before, He can do it again.

Pastor Robin Ricks, Christ Our King Church +++

---

wonder the angels of Heaven are worried about a little visitor's reaction to the glory of God.

Next Alex will enter the Temple and speak to God Himself. On the way, he may speak to other angels, or he may not.

"Alex, when you move about in Heaven—"

"I can move by my own power there. My legs work perfectly in Heaven," he smiles. "On earth, I can't walk or move around, but it's different in Heaven."

How wonderful to know that God's grace offers Alex a place where he can have the full movement he was created to have, as well as a foretaste of the perfection he will one day enjoy!

Even in Heaven Alex doesn't have the perfect "resurrection body" that Paul describes in the New Testament. He is a visitor who still has his earthly body; it's simply free of human wounds there. Alex eagerly anticipates the day when he is in Heaven to stay and will finally receive his heavenly body.

+++

Everyone has a purpose, and Alex's purpose is to spread God's Word. . . . I lost my buddy for a while, but it is worth it because of all the people that will come to Jesus.

Aaron Malarkey,
Alex's brother

Alex converses with God until the Lord tells him the visit is finished. Sometimes other angels are in the meetings, and sometimes it is only God and Alex.

"Alex, do you miss God when you're here?"

"No, Daddy, it's the opposite. I miss God when I am *with* Him, because I know I'm going to be away from Him, and I never want to leave. It's sort of like right now, Daddy. You're getting ready to go to your office, and I'm already starting to miss you. That's how it is when I'm with God. I can't wait until I just get to stay. You can't imagine what it's like to be with God, but to also know you're going to have to leave. That's why when I return from Heaven I usually cry."

Alex also has an ongoing connection with Heaven in his prayer life. A few years ago, when I was wrestling with a particular issue, I did what has become natural to me: I prayed about it. Then, just before leaving to go to work, I asked Alex, "When you are praying today, would you remember to pray for me?"

Alex looked at me with a penetrating gaze and said, "Daddy, I'm always in prayer because part of my brain, through the Holy Spirit, is in constant communication with Heaven. My mouth is for talking to people."

My mind immediately went to the verse in the Bible that says to pray without ceasing (1 Thessalonians 5:17). I had always thought it meant we should pray *a lot*, but somehow Alex's words caused me to better understand the continuous nature of communion the verse is calling us to.

My Meeting with an Angel

Thanks to Alex, talk of the presence of angels, demons, and the devil became commonplace in our home—hardly anything to cause alarm. By the middle of 2006, I thought I had seen and heard just about everything regarding the spiritual realm; nothing could surprise me. We always took these visitations seriously, but they no longer elicited astonishment. Then on a warm summer evening in 2006, Alex said, "Daddy, there is an angel in our house, and he wants to talk with you."

I admit it: I was caught off guard . . .

+++

I went to learn from Alex about God.

Pastor Robin Ricks, pastor
of Christ Our King Church

again, for the thousandth time. Unsure of how to respond, I laughed a little nervously and said, "Wait a minute, Alex, you're the one who's the 'angel boy,' not me!"

Alex looked at me matter-of-factly, completely ignoring my evasion. "It's the angel John who is asking for you."

"His name is John? Can you tell me anything else about him?"

"Well, you've already met him, sort of. He helped the other angels pull you out of the car when we had our accident. There were five angels who carried you, and John was one of them. He's the one who held your head."

"I never knew that, Alex. And he has come back?"

"No, not really. He is here all the time. He follows you around a lot."

Still a bit nervous, I said, "What do you want me to do, Alex?"

"Just look for him, Daddy! He's right here."

"Alex, I can't see angels the way you can." Alex's experience with angels is so familiar to him that he takes it all for granted, often forgetting that others don't see as he sees.

His brow furrowed, and I could tell his mental gears were turning.

"Daddy, what is that word that means you can see through something?"

"Um . . . *transparent*?"

"Yes, Daddy, that's it. Just try to be transparent in your spirit. Then you'll see the angel."

Oh, that's all I had to do, just be transparent *in my spirit*. For Alex, it was as simple as that. But what did that mean? I struggled to get my mind around what Alex was trying to explain, but after a few minutes of intense concentration, all I saw was what everyone with "normal" vision sees upon entering our house—a living room with furniture. I felt spiritually uncoordinated. My son couldn't function in the physical world, but I was handicapped in the spiritual world. Who had the greater disability?

A strong sense of disappointment settled over me. I have learned to trust Alex when he makes these kinds of proclamations, but something was hindering my receiving what God had for me.

"Alex, I need to take out the trash. I'll see you in a few minutes."

Alex, who had been studying my face, sensed my low spirits. "Daddy, don't give up on seeing John, okay?"

Alex always wanted Beth and me to enter the spiritual realm with him—to experience what he experienced and to see what he saw.

"I'll keep trying," I said. "I'll do my best."

Taking the Malarkey trash bins to the street takes effort. Our driveway is about a tenth of a mile long. After walking to the end of the driveway, I paused in the growing dusk. It was a beautiful evening. I waited and listened and heard . . . a chorus of crickets.

I really was trying, because I believed Alex. There were too many times he had spoken into people's lives, too many times he had direct experiences with angels, too many miracles to doubt that God had opened to Alex some rare window into the heavenly realm. Surely if an angel had a message from God to deliver to me, I must have the ability to see or hear it. I slowly lifted my heart and my hands to Heaven. "God, I am here. If You want to say something to me through one of Your angels, I am willing to receive any experience You want me to have."

Some people are physically challenged; I must be supernaturally challenged. Alex must be far beyond me. I looked back toward the house, deeply breathing the night air. Then suddenly I said, "I have anointed you with a message of hope."

Where did that come from? A sudden chill ran over my body as I glanced around. There was nothing out of the ordinary to see, but Someone had just spoken to me in my spirit. A trembling of my spirit gave me the sense there was more. Like a radio signal tuning in to the right frequency, it came first in fits and starts. My heart raced within my chest. The Lord was directly communicating His will for me. I took off running up the driveway and burst through the door. I was all thumbs riffling through the counter and desk, looking for anything to begin writing:

I have anointed you with a message of hope . . .
for the church . . .
the body of Christ . . .
and those who will be the body . . .
that He will be raised up and seen in His true glory . . .
This is the word of the Lord given to you by the angel John.

I dropped the pen and reread what I had just written.

"Alex! Alex!"

Seeing my joyous state, Beth and Aaron gathered around, listening with amazement.

"He spoke to me . . . in my spirit . . . at the end of the driveway. John the angel spoke to me and said . . ." And I read aloud the message I had just received.

Beth and Aaron sat in surprised wonder, but Alex wasn't the least bit moved. If I'd told him the crickets were singing tonight, he would have had the same response—*no big deal, happens all the time*. I was ecstatic, but it was all old hat to him. Just when the rest of us were basking in the warmth of that spiritual afterglow, Alex said, "There's more. You should go back out there."

I went back out to the identical spot—I wasn't going to tamper with anything about this experience. Before long, the voice came again:

Speak of Me, for Me, and about Me
Use Alex to show who I am
I have chosen him as a screen upon which to show Myself
I am unity, the Trinity, a complete circle,
Your story will lead to praise and worship, there will be altar calls
Your bills are the least of My worries
I will be with you all the days of your life
I will speak to you
I will guide you
I am in you
I am about you, you be about Me
My love is unconditional
My vengeance is restricted for the holy
My apostles died for Me, will you die for Me?
I am the Alpha and the Omega, the First and the Last.

Back at the house, I again wrote furiously before hurrying to Alex's room. He had fallen fast asleep. The morning seemed days away. I was so eager to share with him what I had received. When Alex finally woke up, I read to him all that I had written down.

Nonchalant he simply said, "You got all of it."

It was all routine for him, but I felt as if I'd been lifted up, turned upside down, and shaken to my very soul. Please understand, I don't come from a background that regularly embraces supernatural invasions into our physical realm; my faith pilgrimage had been highly conservative. But even in the process of publishing this book, I can see what the Lord revealed to me beginning to be fulfilled.

+++

My grandson's and son's faith in Christ has created a resilience in them that has changed this tragedy into a story of wonderful meaning and purpose for me, my family, and many others.

Dr. William Malarkey,
Kevin's father

Perhaps discussions of another, spiritual realm make you uncomfortable. If so, you're in good company—they make me uncomfortable too. It is one thing for others to have supernatural encounters, quite another when you are the recipient. Nothing even remotely close to this experience had ever occurred in my life. My mind had to struggle to catch up with my spirit. If you don't have a neat theological box in which to put all these things comfortably away, don't worry; neither do I. They are what they are. I am simply reporting what happened. Fortunately we have the Scriptures as an infallible guide to evaluate everything we experience.

The Real Angels

While some people have difficulty contemplating the spiritual realm, others seem to have an unhealthy fascination with heavenly things. It can become a way to avoid either responding to God as He has revealed Himself in the Bible or doing the work of God in the mundane, ordinary days that compose our lives. After all, don't we all have times when we wish we didn't have to clean the bathroom? As much love as there is in my family, there are some days when I would like to be transported away from my duties and lie on a sunny beach contemplating angels!

Heaven, angels, and miracles are wonderful and fascinating. If all Alex and I have done is provided a momentary thrill through telling what has happened in our lives, though, we have failed most miserably. The Bible clearly speaks against those who worship the creation rather than the Creator. In the same way, if we aren't careful, we can become enamored of the messengers and miss the God who created and sent them.

Angels are not cute little cherubs who live on the limbs of Christmas trees; they are powerful created beings to do the work of God. The Bible constantly describes the angels as God's messengers and special agents, crossing over into the physical world to carry out His assignments. The Bible also tells us to be hospitable since we may one day entertain angels without realizing it, as others have done (Hebrews 13:2).

If I may offer a humble word of exhortation, the enemy is a deceiver who masquerades as an angel of light. We all need to be on guard against counterfeit truth. Anything that doesn't square with Scripture is counterfeit. Alex's angels never operate outside the parameters we find in Scripture—the measure of authenticity.

You don't need to see or talk with angels to live a life that glorifies God. Don't be derailed in your quest for meaning by seeking a supernatural experience. Seek God through His Son, Jesus Christ.

Alex's hope is that upon hearing how God has revealed Himself in Alex's life, you will be drawn to the only One who provides true hope.

From Alex
I Still Visit Heaven

Then as I looked, I saw a door standing open in heaven.

REVELATION 4:1

I don't really like talking about Heaven very much these days. I liked it better telling my mommy and daddy things when they were new experiences for me. I was excited to share what I was seeing. I know God has a purpose for my car accident and for what He has shown me in Heaven. I know that all of this can help other people. But it's hard to talk about heavenly things. They are harder to describe than things on earth. I don't have all the words I need.

When Daddy starts asking me questions now, I usually roll my eyes and try to get to the last question. When we're done, I'm hoping for a video game or some time just to play with Daddy.

Last night my daddy shared with me that sometimes God wants us to share what He shows us, and sometimes He wants us to keep it to ourselves. He told me how the apostle Paul was told not to tell what he had seen in Heaven. Daddy told me that God told John the opposite: that he should share what he was shown in Heaven—or at least some of it.

This made me feel relieved. I believe that I am a combination of John and Paul. I know that I need to share some of what I have seen in Heaven, and I also know that God has told me not to tell about other things. I am allowed to tell my parents some things that they are not allowed to share, and some things I do not even tell them.

God knows exactly what I can handle. He knows how much I can understand, and He knows what would be too hard for me to keep from sharing. He is perfect!

One night my dad said he believed I was only sharing about 10 percent of what I have seen in Heaven. This put a big smile on my face.

Still, I wasn't sure if I should share all of this in a book. I asked my daddy about it, and I told him that I don't want people making a big deal about me. But I've decided that it's okay to share some things because, after all, Heaven and angels are a part of the Bible's message. I hope it will bring people closer to God.

So I will tell you a little more.

When I visit Heaven, I see angels flying around the throne of God. They are singing as they fly.

I thought that the two wings over the angels' faces were masks, but later when my daddy and I talked about it, I realized they were wings.

Does the Bible tell how the angel Michael is next to the throne, writing down what people do on earth?

I know I am with God when I am visiting Heaven, but you can't see God on His throne—the angels fly so fast that they block Him from view.

Nobody gets to see God's face until later.

CHAPTER 10

THE ROAD AHEAD

*When people ask me if my faith is shaken because Alex
hasn't been fully healed, I respond with a confident no.
The last two years have brought new, amazing reminders
that we are still held in the palm of God's hand.*

AFTER ALL OUR confident assertions about Alex's full recovery,
wouldn't it be great to end the book with a story about Alex waking
up one morning miraculously healed, leaping out of bed, and rac-
ing to the front lawn to play football with Aaron or climb trees with
Gracie? But reality is more complex—more beautiful than that.

While Alex's injuries restrict him in some ways, he has the same
goals, dreams, and aspirations of any young man whose heart belongs
to God. And he has the determination to pursue them!

The New Normal

For Alex, this means hard work—both physical and mental—every
day. Alex is a trouper. Beth leads him through a one-hour stretching session each morning and evening to ensure that his limbs and
torso remain limber. Beth provides all of Alex's stretching therapy,

and she cleans Alex's trach tube site during each stretching session as well. Two times per week, a physical therapist comes to take Alex through different body movements using a variety of sophisticated equipment, some of which simulate walking.

We homeschool our children, as we had begun to do even before the accident. Alex loves reading and spends part of each school day working through several courses at an online charter school. He uses his mouth to control a mouse while navigating through his math course and other studies. The accident set Alex back an entire year academically, but he has already made up that year and is now at grade level.

Alex loves to attend church and even sings in the choir. If he is well and can make it, on Sunday mornings you will find him at Christ Our King Church. He is highly social and never misses the opportunity to interact with people. Alex loves dishing it out and has a reputation for getting the last word!

Alex can operate his wheelchair by moving his chin. He loves playing duck, duck, goose and hide-and-seek. (He usually does the seeking, but when it is his turn to hide, we cover him with blankets and pillows in an inconspicuous spot.) He also loves to play video games. Aaron and I are the "hands" and Alex is the "brains" when we play: "Turn here; no, slow down! Right, go right!" Alex even plays with Nerf guns. We dress him up in goggles and a chest protector and lay a Nerf gun across his lap, and he tries to run over the other players with his wheelchair.

As already mentioned, Alex is a total sports buff and can keep pace with the best informed. He is a fierce defender of his favorite teams and never misses games. When Alex heard that President Obama had picked Georgetown to upset the Bucks in the 2010 men's basketball tournament, he had a thing or two to say about it. But what would you expect from a kid whose dad manipulated the system to have his son born in the hospital room with the best view of the Buckeyes' stadium?

+++ When situations arise—and "many are the afflictions of the righteous" (Psalm 34:19, KJV)—God gives us His grace in proportion to our needs. Jesus Christ ministers gracefully to all who trust in Him.

I think about what the apostle Paul said after listing some of the things he had endured—he spent a day and a night in the deep, he was among false brethren, he was beaten—but then he said, "Most gladly therefore will I rather glory in my infirmities, that the power of Christ may rest upon me" (2 Corinthians 12:9, KJV). So why would Paul glory in his infirmities? Because it is there that the power of God rested on him. Through his trials, a greater measure of the Lord's grace was realized.

And so the real question is not, What is it like to be in a wheelchair? The question is, What is God like when you're in a wheelchair? That's the real question, because He does give abundant grace.

Pastor Robin Ricks, Christ Our King Church +++

Occasionally someone will say to Beth or me, "How do you do it? I could never do that." Well, when God gives you something to do, you just do it. What seems foreign to someone else is normal for us. Every one of us will, to some degree or another, be faced with a new normal sometime in life. When we embrace it and carry on, we tend to be a lot happier.

On one level, then, our family has developed new daily rhythms, and we enjoy play and laughter as much as any other. Yet that doesn't mean we've resigned ourselves to things as they are now. God is still at work, advancing His purposes in our family's and Alex's lives. The last two years have brought new, amazing reminders that we are still held in the palm of His hand.

St. Louis

As Alex's story continues to unfold, we can only thank God for the ongoing interest and support that has enabled him to make great strides forward. Beth has done an immense amount of research regarding Alex's development. It was a long-standing dream to have him admitted into the Kennedy Krieger Institute (KKI) in Baltimore for their two-week program. KKI is the world's premier institution for the treatment of children just like Alex. This facility offered the same type of therapy and treatment that Christopher Reeve received. But there was always a major obstacle—the $15,000 price tag for the treatment program. Now this isn't a lot of money to God, but for us it was a mountain too high to climb. If Alex was going to go to the KKI, God would have to provide.

In the course of Beth's research, she met Patrick Rummerfield, who works for the International Center for Spinal Cord Injury at KKI. Patrick's interest in spinal cord research is personal. In 1974 he survived a car accident but was rendered a quadriplegic. He worked extremely hard through physical therapy and eventually recovered the full use of his limbs. In fact, he is the only fully recovered quadriplegic in the world. Today, Patrick races marathons all over the world. Beth has worked tirelessly to get Alex to KKI since shortly after the accident, and Patrick has worked right alongside her from the beginning.

In July 2009, the KKI dream was made a reality through the great generosity of many people. The first is Eric Westacott. In 1993, Eric was sliding headfirst toward home during an intramural college softball game and became a quadriplegic. This didn't stop Eric. Today he is an attorney as well as the president of the Eric Westacott Foundation. He drives his own van, works full-time, and, more importantly, is a fantastic human being. His positive outlook is powerful, and the way he works tirelessly for others is truly inspiring. Every year Eric's foundation hosts a golf tournament in St. Louis whose sole purpose is to raise funds to benefit spinal cord research. In 2009, the tournament proceeds were designated for rehabilitative efforts for Alex, specifically to send him to the KKI.

Eric and Patrick worked together to hold the golf tournament and silent auction for Alex. The Eric Westacott Foundation sent the funds for our family to travel to St. Louis for a week. This was exciting for all of us. We had not all traveled or spent any nights away from home together since 2004. We would drive the van paid for by our church, pull a trailer lent to us by a family whose son with a spinal cord injury had recently passed away, and travel with money provided by the Westacott Foundation.

When we arrived in St. Louis, Eric and Patrick gave us tickets to attend a Cardinals baseball game the next day. Alex and Aaron love baseball. It was the first time we had the opportunity to take Alex to a game. It was great fun. We went two hours early to watch batting practice, and we did our best to break the concession-stand spending record for a single game!

On Saturday we went to the sixteenth annual EWF Golf Classic Tournament. People fly in from around the country to participate. We had no direct connection with any of these people. It was humbling to watch all the effort that had gone into helping Alex.

During the banquet and silent auction, we had fun watching friends attempt to outbid each other to help Alex. Alex was introduced and received a standing ovation, and Patrick and Beth followed with short speeches. Finally, a giant check was brought out and presented to Alex. The Eric Westacott Foundation had raised twice the amount required for a two-week stay at the KKI. Alex would now be able to go for two separate two-week stays.

In a sense, my family and I were spectators that evening. We were the recipients of the foundation's efforts, but we truly were among strangers. It was amazing to me that people who did not even know us could be so generous. Their attitudes were consistent with the kindness we had experienced from the church. God can use anyone to further His purposes. Jesus is always showing Himself through every situation, if only we are willing to see.

In addition to all his efforts with Eric and his foundation, Patrick also contacted the Christopher and Dana Reeve Foundation and asked them to help in yet another way. We had for several years been trying to acquire a specialized rehabilitation bike for Alex. Lorraine Valentini, a U.S. cycling champion, and her husband, Chris Reyling, had donated the exact bike that Alex needed to the Reeves' foundation. The RT300 Functional Electrical Stimulation (FES) bike is designed to send electrical impulses to electrodes placed on the person's muscles, causing the muscles to contract and basically perform a workout. Patrick was directly instrumental in acquiring this bike for Alex. Again, the generosity was amazing, our God, awesome.

Supernatural Awakening

Alex's supernatural awakening to the most powerful and peaceful reality known to anyone happened when he was only six years old. Since then, his experience has been like that of a character in a movie who keeps enjoying a lavish heavenly banquet only to be jolted back every twenty minutes into scenes of family life and great physical hardship—before the final scene where everything comes full circle!

God has given Alex special grace to walk his own pilgrimage, creating an unusually beautiful and pure relationship with the Spirit of God. Alex's body is not where we wish it were, but his spirit is far beyond where we could have ever imagined when we prayed, at his birth, that our son would walk closely with God.

Don't misunderstand. This doesn't mean that Alex is some other-worldly saint. Far from it, at times. He's a normal twelve-year-old who loves practical jokes and sports, who at times is disobedient to his mom and dad, and who happens to be in a wheelchair.

+++ One conversation with Alex can completely change a person's mind-set and perspective of life. This is a testimony of how God is working greatly through his life and of his personal passion for Jesus. I have had talks with this young man that made me feel my faith is somewhere behind doubting Thomas's! It is inspiring faith. But as deep as Alex is—and I could spend all day talking with him about God and what he has experienced—it is refreshing to know he acts like any other twelve-year-old, in need of correction and all.

Will Zell, pastor of evangelism, Christ Our King Church +++

Superman and Surgery

In 2003 world-renowned surgeon and researcher Dr. Raymond Onders installed a small device in Christopher Reeve that allowed him to breathe without a ventilator. In January 2009 Alex was scheduled to receive what many call the "Christopher Reeve surgery."

+++

Mr. Matt, when you and my dad go to meet with the publisher people, tell them I'm just a normal kid and be sure to tell them I'm ornery.

Alex Malarkey, speaking to
Matt Jacobson, literary agent
for Kevin and Alex Malarkey

Christopher Reeve led the way for adults. Alex would lead the way for children, as he would be the first child in the world to undergo Dr. Onders's groundbreaking surgery. The operation involves implanting a small device that allows paralyzed patients to breathe without a ventilator by stimulating the muscles and nerves that run through the body's diaphragm. In June 2008, the Food and Drug Administration approved the device for use in adults. University Hospitals in Cleveland got special permission from the FDA to perform the surgery on Alex.

Just prior to the surgery, we received a call from the public relations department at the hospital about the possibility of some media covering the procedure. "Sure," we agreed, imagining a press release or perhaps a local news story. Surely we could provide a quick interview after all that was being done for us. We underestimated the media attention Alex's surgery would engender by . . . just a little.

Beth, Alex, and I arrived in Cleveland the night before the surgery to take care of all the preliminary work at the hospital. We began completing paperwork and the minor pre-op tests. Before long, several reporters arrived from Cleveland's *Plain Dealer* newspaper and a few television stations. We spoke with the reporters, but for some reason we didn't ask ourselves, *Why is the press arriving the night before Alex's surgery?*

The next morning, I thumbed through the back pages of the *Plain Dealer* to see if there was an article. Finding nothing, I folded and tossed the paper on the counter before doing a double take. There was a major story on Alex on the front page of the paper. The front page? He hadn't even had the surgery yet! It was a well-done article, although all the references we had made to God in the interview had been removed. (The writer later apologized to me for that. The original copy the reporter supplied to the paper had the actual interview, as it took place. An editor at the paper removed the references to God. I hope he or she reads this book!)

When we were driving to the hospital later that morning, I made a wrong turn. That pushed back our arrival time by a few minutes and gave the media crowd more time to gather. When we walked through the doors into the pre-op area, we discovered that about twenty media people with elaborate lighting systems had already set up their equipment, ready to begin filming. The morning started with a round of presurgery interviews with Beth, Dr. Onders, and me. At one point I went out to the lobby to get a cup of coffee. No sooner had I entered the room than a woman said to me, "Cleveland is praying for your

+++

Christopher Reeve led the way. Chris had the courage to be one of our first patients and led the way for successful outpatient laparoscopic diaphragm pacing system with a home-based ventilator weaning program.

Dr. Raymond Onders, quoted at www.synapsebiomedical.com/ news/reeve son." I was taken aback, again not aware of the massive interest in my son's surgery.

"Oh, I am sorry," she said. "Did you know you were on all of the morning newscasts?"

"No, I didn't."

"Well, you were. Everyone is talking about it. My church is keeping Alex in their prayers."

Amid all the media activity and general business surrounding a major operation, I was keeping a close eye on Alex. I could see that following the preparation for surgery, he was feeling a little nervous. Dr. Onders could tell too. He's a consummate professional who is highly attuned to his patients. Before long, Alex and Dr. Onders were talking smack about football. Alex made it clear that his Steelers were better than Dr. Onders's Browns. Minutes later, Alex was wheeled into surgery.

Beth and I were not allowed past a certain point, but a man with a camera was. He filmed the entire surgery, while members of the media congregated in the hallway. Beth and I gave interviews during most of the ninety minutes that Alex was out of our sight. It was actually a wonderful distraction for us. Busy with endless reporters' questions, we had little time to worry about Alex. Toward the end of the surgery, I noticed one of the reporters off by herself, praying. Beth and I made our way over to her, and the three of us were soon praying together.

Finally people began to leave the operating room, and soon after that Alex was wheeled out. He looked fine, with the exception of the electrical wire sticking out of his upper chest to which the external device would be plugged in. It felt a bit strange to see our child wired for an electrical current!

We were eager to hear from Dr. Onders and to get his perspective on the surgery.

"Everything went very well. The surgery was a success," he began. "In fact, when I hooked up the device for a test run in the operating room, Alex took such a deep breath, he almost blew his chest out! Normally, we test the system for five minutes. With Alex, we tested for a full fifteen minutes. Everything went very well."

We were thrilled.

Alex was rolled into the post-op area, where reporters waited in anticipation. Even before Alex had regained consciousness, various newscasters were conducting live reports for their organizations. Beth and I stood smiling next to the bed, dutifully following our instructions to stare down at Alex as the reporter talked about him.

With the cameras running, Dr. Onders walked over to Alex and said, "All during surgery, I was saying, 'Go Browns!'"

Alex hadn't fully regained consciousness. Even so, he was lucid enough to whisper in a faint voice, "The Steelers are in the play-offs, not the Browns."

That's Alex—always quick on the comeback, even if he is only half conscious!

In the swirl of media activity, we didn't know what was next, so we were somewhat surprised when a schedule was pressed into our hands—our media appearance schedule, that is. Alex, it was explained, would need several hours to recover; in the meantime, we would be giving interviews. Isn't that what we had agreed to do? Associated Press at 2:00, the Cleveland *Plain Dealer* at 2:30, etc. I had to ask myself, Which was more strange: that (a) the surgery to help my son breathe on his own was an outpatient procedure, or (b) we were being released from the hospital based on our media schedule?

The interviews went well, but not without at least one awkward moment. A television reporter seemed to relish the opportunity to have a direct interview with Alex.

"So, Alex, now that your ventilator can be removed at times and you can breathe with this new device, do you feel normal?"

Alex looked at her with intense eyes, a confused expression spreading over his face.

"What do you mean?" He paused for a moment then continued, "I *am* normal."

The reporter was mortified for wandering into forbidden territory and apologized profusely. Alex spent the next few minutes making sure *she* felt better.

Another reporter with the Associated Press listened as his interview was consumed with my half-conscious son rambling on about the Pittsburgh Steelers. The reporter didn't seem to mind. He then said something that caught me off guard. "You should write a book."

"You really think so?"

"Yes, I do."

"Do you have any specific advice about the process?" I asked.

"Yes. Work hard and never be discouraged. That's it."

Good advice for just about everything in life, I thought. It was on this day that I made the decision to write a book about Alex and his experiences. I had thought about it before, but that AP reporter's encouragement was the beginning of the book you now hold in your hand.

We then did one more newspaper interview and headed down to the van. Accompanying us, the reporter from this interview assured us that she would include aspects of faith in her piece because she knew it was an integral part of the story.

The big article on Alex appeared in the newspaper the following

day—lots of column inches and several excellent pictures. God . . . ?
No, He wasn't mentioned.

We made our way back to the hotel, and the phone rang. It was
my mother.

"Hey, Mom, good to hear from you. Everything went great. Alex
is a champ."

"Yes, I know," she said. "Alex looks great."

"You're two hundred miles away. How do you know Alex looks
great?"

"Oh, the pictures of the surgery and post-op are all over the
Internet. He really does look great. Maybe when you get back to the
hotel, you can Google Alex and see what I'm talking about."

Does this not say something about the times we live in? We
weren't even home from the hospital, and my parents, hundreds of
miles away, had seen what went on in the operating room before I
had! I did Google Alex when we arrived back at the hotel. There were
more than four pages of entries. Incredible!

We intended to go home the next day but were snowed in and
forced to stay another day in Cleveland. While this was a nice gift in
that it gave the three of us a day to do nothing but relax, it also made
the drive home a bit more hectic.

We *had* to get home in time for the kickoff of the Steelers' first
playoff game against the San Diego Chargers!

Stiffening the Spine: The Young Man Who Is Alex

Anyone who has spoken with Alex will testify that one thing Alex
doesn't lack is spine. His physical spine suffered from atrophied back
muscles and was badly curved, but when it comes to the spine that
really counts—strength of spirit—Alex has no lack. This boldness,

+++

Alex is one amazing kid. You start out thinking that he probably needs encouragement, being confined to a wheelchair. Then you start a conversation with him, and immediately it's the other way around. Alex lifts your spirits! He encourages you! That's just Alex.

Dan Tullis

coupled with what he has seen and continues to experience of the heavenly world, has molded Alex into a dynamic witness for Jesus Christ. If you meet Alex, you're going to hear the gospel.

To help Alex sit properly in his chair and fully benefit from Dr. Onders's "Christopher Reeve surgery," his doctors determined that Alex would need to have steel rods attached to his spinal column. On December 1, 2009, Beth and I filled our fifteen-passenger van with medical equipment for Alex as well as Beth's suitcase, anticipating that the two of them would stay in Cleveland for two weeks while Alex recuperated.

The night before the surgery, Alex's spirit was light, and we all had a great time joking around and hanging out at our hotel. But as morning came and we walked through pre-op procedures, Alex grew increasingly nervous. He asked a series of questions about what the surgery would entail, and then turning to me, terror marring his face, he said, "Daddy, I am afraid I am going to die."

I'd had that same fear all week, but of course I hadn't breathed a hint of it to him. Now where would I find words to comfort him? I gathered myself and said, "Alex, if you do, you'll be home, and if not, we'll move on with life."

It's hardly surprising that my comment brought him no peace. As we rolled Alex down the hallway, he became agitated and slurred his words. The nurses assured us he would not remember going down the hall.

We were told surgery would take between five and eight hours. Beth chose to pass this time in the waiting room. I walked restlessly through the grounds surrounding the hospital. Beth had a pager. I had a cell phone. We were nervous. Alex's spine was curved at an 89-degree angle, and he had to be cut open from the base of his neck down to his hips.

The surgeons gave us progress updates a few times. They finished in about four hours. At one point, Dr. Onders showed up to tell us he had just checked on Alex. Three people were sewing Alex up, he explained, and this would take about an hour. When the surgery was done, we were informed that it had been a tremendous success. Alex's spine was now perfectly straight, and he was recovering in the ICU.

Alex was awake when we first saw him, but he was pretty out of it. Beth stayed with him in the ICU, and I returned to the hotel. I returned in the morning to make sure Beth and Alex were okay and then headed back home to be with the other three kids.

Due to complications, Alex had to spend the next three weeks in the ICU recovering from his surgery. During this time Beth stayed with him every night, rarely leaving the room. What Alex experienced physically for the next fifteen days almost defies description. Alex's Army was praying. It was a battle of titanic proportions. At one point, Alex lost his vision. He had tremendous problems getting air, and his blood pressure repeatedly switched between extreme highs and extreme lows. Alex's words came out as a faint whisper. Several times, he was sure his fears about dying were coming true.

As trying as this time was for Alex, we were reasonably confident that he would pull through. The medical staff worked mightily to stabilize him, even as he failed to improve for many days. At one point during this time, the team of doctors and other medical staff—about eight people—assembled around Alex's bed to collaborate. Alex's flaccid body was flat on the bed, he was extremely weak, and his vitals were unstable. He continued to have problems breathing. In his compromised condition, Alex had only one thing on his mind. He lifted weary eyes to look at the medical team and in his now feeble, whispering voice asked, "Do any of you have a personal relationship with God?"

"I do," one person said. The rest of them exchanged quick glances.

Alex then began to talk about Jesus to the rest of the medical team. He never once mentioned himself or his own circumstances. He was only concerned about the other people and their relationship with God through Jesus. Because he had so little breath, Beth would lean down, listen, and then act as Alex's interpreter. When he was finished, one of the medical people smiled and said, "Alex, you are amazing."

Alex responded, "*God* is amazing. I'm just a kid."

+++

Every time I leave Alex after spending a little time talking with him, I ask myself, "Why don't I ever feel sorry for him?"

Rachael,
friend of the Malarkeys

Over the next week Beth continued to give me updates as Alex talked about God with virtually every person who entered his room. One day a nurse came in when Alex was too exhausted to speak. He looked at his mother and said, "You tell her."

When Alex finally returned home from Cleveland following a 180-mile ambulance ride, I asked, "Alex, did you tell everyone you saw about Jesus?"

Alex smiled and said, "Daddy, please. Of course I did!"

This is why, when people ask me if my faith is shaken because Alex hasn't been fully healed, I can respond with a firm no. Certainly Alex is going to be fully healed, whether here on earth or in Heaven. How that occurs is God's choice, yet I am totally convinced that his healing will occur in this life.

God has touched so many lives and brought so much good out of Alex's pilgrimage that I know God is not only directing His plan, but He is also directing the timing of His plan. That's where our confident hope rests.

And . . . It Isn't Over Yet!

Afterword:
Questions and Answers with Alex

Q: What do you know about a current Heaven and a future Heaven on earth?

A: I know that there is a place other than the one I go to. The angel Ryan told me that the future Heaven is where you get the new bodies. He wishes that he could have one of those bodies.

Q: Do you hear talk of the New Heaven where you are?

A: The other Heaven is there now, but in a different place.

Q: Is the Garden of Eden and/or the tree of life in the present Heaven?

A: I have no idea.

Q: Are there cities in Heaven?

A: Yes. They make New York City seem small! The skyline is awesome.

Q: What was your body like in Heaven?

A: I never really paid attention to my body. I never looked down or thought about myself. I was too in awe of everything else. I know that I could walk in Heaven, though.

Q: What do you think about the fact that God told Paul not to talk about what he saw in Heaven, but He told John to share about his visit?

A: I don't feel so weird when I think about that. I'm a mixture of the two. Some things I can say and some things I can't.

Q: Have you ever seen hell (from Heaven or at any other time)?

A: I've never seen hell myself. There is the hole that I told you about in outer Heaven. I know that if you go through that hole, you end up in hell. This makes me very sad.

Q: What is worship like in Heaven?

A: It's always happening. The angels have sessions of praising God. They go to His throne at certain times. I have seen the elders bowing down and saying, "Holy, holy, holy." But the most awesome part is the angels behind the elders. There are more than you can count.

Q: What people have you seen in Heaven?

A: I have seen people from the Bible. I cannot say anything else.

Q: Is Heaven a physical place?

A: How could I have been there if it wasn't?

Q: If you were going to speak to a group of young people about prayer, what would you tell them?

A: I would have fun and tell them the truth. God loves you, and He is always there. I would then describe God's love and His presence. I would want them to know that He hears you when you are praying and He loves you.

Q: What would you tell people about spiritual warfare?

A: I would only have three main points. (1) Satan is a loser, and he has already lost; (2) demons are trying to mess with people nonstop; (3) we need Jesus in our hearts to fight the demons.

Q: If the president of the United States was on the phone with you, what would you tell him?

A: Let God be your leader. Follow God and try to get people to follow Him. If you do this, nothing evil can mess with you. And by the way, Georgetown stinks. Go Bucks!

Q: What would you say to someone who is troubled or anxious?

A: If they are, I would just say, "Ask God for help."

Scripture Appendix

Angels

For he will order his angels
   to protect you wherever you go.
They will hold you up with their hands
   so you won't even hurt your foot on a stone.   PSALM 91:11-12

There is joy in the presence of God's angels when even one sinner
repents.   LUKE 15:10

Angels are only servants—spirits sent to care for people who will
inherit salvation.   HEBREWS 1:14

For in one place the Scriptures say,
   "What are mere mortals that you should think about them,
      or a son of man that you should care for him?
   Yet you made them only a little lower than the angels
      and crowned them with glory and honor."   HEBREWS 2:6-7

*Don't forget to show hospitality to strangers, for some who have done
this have entertained angels without realizing it!*   HEBREWS 13:2

*They were told that their messages were not for themselves, but for
you. And now this Good News has been announced to you by those
who preached in the power of the Holy Spirit sent from heaven. It
is all so wonderful that even the angels are eagerly watching these
things happen.*   1 PETER 1:12

*And all the angels were standing around the throne and around the
elders and the four living beings. And they fell before the throne with
their faces to the ground and worshiped God. They sang,*
  "Amen! Blessing and glory and wisdom
    and thanksgiving and honor
  and power and strength belong to our God
    forever and ever! Amen."   REVELATION 7:11-12

God's Care for Children

*But God heard the boy crying, and the angel of God called to Hagar
from heaven, "Hagar, what's wrong? Do not be afraid! God has heard
the boy crying as he lies there. Go to him and comfort him, for I will
make a great nation from his descendants."*   GENESIS 21:17-18

And you must commit yourselves wholeheartedly to these commands that I am giving you today. Repeat them again and again to your children. Talk about them when you are at home and when you are on the road, when you are going to bed and when you are getting up. Tie them to your hands and wear them on your forehead as reminders. Write them on the doorposts of your house and on your gates.

DEUTERONOMY 6:6-9

You have taught children and infants
  to tell of your strength,
silencing your enemies
  and all who oppose you. PSALM 8:2

For he will conceal me there when troubles come;
  he will hide me in his sanctuary.
  He will place me out of reach on a high rock. PSALM 27:5

We will not hide these truths from our children;
  we will tell the next generation
about the glorious deeds of the LORD,
  about his power and his mighty wonders. PSALM 78:4

The LORD is like a father to his children,
  tender and compassionate to those who fear him. PSALM 103:13

Children are a gift from the LORD;
they are a reward from him.   PSALM 127:3

Direct your children onto the right path,
and when they are older, they will not leave it.   PROVERBS 22:6

I knew you before I formed you in your mother's womb.
Before you were born I set you apart.   JEREMIAH 1:5

At that time Jesus prayed this prayer: "O Father, Lord of heaven
and earth, thank you for hiding these things from those who think
themselves wise and clever, and for revealing them to the childlike.
Yes, Father, it pleased you to do it this way!"   MATTHEW 11:25-26

About that time the disciples came to Jesus and asked, "Who is greatest
in the Kingdom of Heaven?"
Jesus called a little child to him and put the child among them.
Then he said, "I tell you the truth, unless you turn from your sins and
become like little children, you will never get into the Kingdom of
Heaven. So anyone who becomes as humble as this little child is the
greatest in the Kingdom of Heaven.
"And anyone who welcomes a little child like this on my behalf
is welcoming me. But if you cause one of these little ones who trusts in
me to fall into sin, it would be better for you to have a large millstone
tied around your neck and be drowned in the depths of the sea."
MATTHEW 18:1-6

The leading priests and the teachers of religious law saw these wonderful miracles and heard even the children in the Temple shouting, "Praise God for the Son of David."

But the leaders were indignant. They asked Jesus, "Do you hear what these children are saying?"

"Yes," Jesus replied. "Haven't you ever read the Scriptures? For they say, 'You have taught children and infants to give you praise.'"

MATTHEW 21:15-16

One day some parents brought their children to Jesus so he could touch and bless them. But the disciples scolded the parents for bothering him.

When Jesus saw what was happening, he was angry with his disciples. He said to them, "Let the children come to me. Don't stop them! For the Kingdom of God belongs to those who are like these children. I tell you the truth, anyone who doesn't receive the Kingdom of God like a child will never enter it." Then he took the children in his arms and placed his hands on their heads and blessed them.

MARK 10:13-16

To all who believed him and accepted him, he gave the right to become children of God. JOHN 1:12

Don't let anyone think less of you because you are young. Be an example to all believers in what you say, in the way you live, in your love, your faith, and your purity. I TIMOTHY 4:12

*Have you forgotten the encouraging words God spoke to you as his
children? He said,*

> *"My child, don't make light of the LORD's discipline,*
>> *and don't give up when he corrects you.*
> *For the LORD disciplines those he loves,*
>> *and he punishes each one he accepts as his child."*

*As you endure this divine discipline, remember that God is treating you
as his own children. Who ever heard of a child who is never disciplined
by its father? If God doesn't discipline you as he does all of his children,
it means that you are illegitimate and are not really his children at all.
Since we respected our earthly fathers who disciplined us, shouldn't we
submit even more to the discipline of the Father of our spirits, and live
forever?* HEBREWS 12:5-9

Heaven

> *You will show me the way of life,*
>> *granting me the joy of your presence*
>> *and the pleasures of living with you forever.* PSALM 16:11

> *Surely your goodness and unfailing love will pursue me*
>> *all the days of my life,*
> *and I will live in the house of the LORD*
>> *forever.* PSALM 23:6

It was in the year King Uzziah died that I saw the Lord. He was sitting on a lofty throne, and the train of his robe filled the Temple. Attending him were mighty seraphim, each having six wings. With two wings they covered their faces, with two they covered their feet, and with two they flew. They were calling out to each other,
> *"Holy, holy, holy is the LORD of Heaven's Armies!*
> *The whole earth is filled with his glory!"* ISAIAH 6:1-3

Pray like this:
> *Our Father in heaven,*
> > *may your name be kept holy.*
> *May your Kingdom come soon.*
> *May your will be done on earth,*
> > *as it is in heaven.* MATTHEW 6:9-10

Don't store up treasures here on earth, where moths eat them and rust destroys them, and where thieves break in and steal. Store your treasures in heaven, where moths and rust cannot destroy, and thieves do not break in and steal. Wherever your treasure is, there the desires of your heart will also be. MATTHEW 6:19-21

Jesus replied, "The Kingdom of God can't be detected by visible signs. You won't be able to say, 'Here it is!' or 'It's over there!' For the Kingdom of God is already among you." LUKE 17:20-21

Don't let your hearts be troubled. Trust in God, and trust also in me. There is more than enough room in my Father's home. If this were not so, would I have told you that I am going to prepare a place for you? When everything is ready, I will come and get you, so that you will always be with me where I am. And you know the way to where I am going. . . . I am the way, the truth, and the life. No one can come to the Father except through me." JOHN 14:1-4, 6

Against its will, all creation was subjected to God's curse. But with eager hope, the creation looks forward to the day when it will join God's children in glorious freedom from death and decay. For we know that all creation has been groaning as in the pains of childbirth right up to the present time. And we believers also groan, even though we have the Holy Spirit within us as a foretaste of future glory, for we long for our bodies to be released from sin and suffering. We, too, wait with eager hope for the day when God will give us our full rights as his adopted children, including the new bodies he has promised us. ROMANS 8:20-23

What I am saying, dear brothers and sisters, is that our physical bodies cannot inherit the Kingdom of God. These dying bodies cannot inherit what will last forever.

But let me reveal to you a wonderful secret. We will not all die, but we will all be transformed! It will happen in a moment, in the blink of an eye, when the last trumpet is blown. For when the trumpet sounds, those who have died will be raised to live forever. And we who are living will also be transformed. For our dying bodies must be transformed into bodies that will never die; our mortal bodies must be transformed into immortal bodies. 1 CORINTHIANS 15:50-53

For we know that when this earthly tent we live in is taken down (that is, when we die and leave this earthly body), we will have a house in heaven, an eternal body made for us by God himself and not by human hands. We grow weary in our present bodies, and we long to put on our heavenly bodies like new clothing. For we will put on heavenly bodies; we will not be spirits without bodies. While we live in these earthly bodies, we groan and sigh, but it's not that we want to die and get rid of these bodies that clothe us. Rather, we want to put on our new bodies so that these dying bodies will be swallowed up by life. God himself has prepared us for this, and as a guarantee he has given us his Holy Spirit.

So we are always confident, even though we know that as long as we live in these bodies we are not at home with the Lord. For we live by believing and not by seeing. Yes, we are fully confident, and we would rather be away from these earthly bodies, for then we will be at home with the Lord. 2 CORINTHIANS 5:1-8

But we are citizens of heaven, where the Lord Jesus Christ lives. And we are eagerly waiting for him to return as our Savior. He will take our weak mortal bodies and change them into glorious bodies like his own, using the same power with which he will bring everything under his control. PHILIPPIANS 3:20-21

You have come to Mount Zion, to the city of the living God, the heavenly Jerusalem, and to countless thousands of angels in a joyful gathering. HEBREWS 12:22

I heard a loud shout from the throne, saying, "Look, God's home is now among his people! He will live with them, and they will be his people. God himself will be with them. He will wipe every tear from their eyes, and there will be no more death or sorrow or crying or pain. All these things are gone forever." REVELATION 21:3-4

So [one of the seven angels] took me in the Spirit to a great, high mountain, and he showed me the holy city, Jerusalem, descending out of heaven from God. It shone with the glory of God and sparkled like a precious stone—like jasper as clear as crystal. The city wall was broad and high, with twelve gates guarded by twelve angels. And the names of the twelve tribes of Israel were written on the gates. There were three gates on each side—east, north, south, and west. The wall of the city had twelve foundation stones, and on them were written the names of the twelve apostles of the Lamb. . . .

The wall was made of jasper, and the city was pure gold, as clear as glass. The wall of the city was built on foundation stones inlaid with twelve precious stones: the first was jasper, the second sapphire, the third agate, the fourth emerald, the fifth onyx, the sixth carnelian, the seventh chrysolite, the eighth beryl, the ninth topaz, the tenth chrysoprase, the eleventh jacinth, the twelfth amethyst.

The twelve gates were made of pearls—each gate from a single pearl! And the main street was pure gold, as clear as glass.

REVELATION 21:10-14, 18-21

Discussion Questions

Introduction

1. Describe Heaven as you understand it. What forms the basis of your understanding?

2. What does the author mean when he says, "There is an unseen world at work—an intensely active spiritual dimension right here on earth, all around us. And much of this activity keeps us from focusing on our future destination" (pages x–xi)? How does this relate to what you've observed in your own life?

3. What is your initial reaction to Alex's story? to other stories of supernatural experiences?

4. What are you hoping to learn from following "Alex on his journey to Heaven and back"?

Chapter 1: At the Crossroads

1. Describe the tension Kevin feels at the beginning of this chapter—between joy and responsibility, thankfulness and debt. How does this affect Kevin's life and the life of his family? Have you experienced this tension? Explain.

2. What was your response to Pastor Gary Brown's sermon? What significance does God's name Jehovah-jireh ("the LORD will provide") have for you?

3. What was your reaction to Kevin's description of the car wreck and the first minutes after the accident? Can you see evidence of God's mercy even then? If so, explain.

4. Does Alex's perspective help you better understand the accident? Explain.

Chapter 2: Three Journeys

1. Describe Kevin's anguish caused by having to wait at the local hospital knowing his son has been flown elsewhere. Can you relate to how Kevin was feeling? Explain.

2. Discuss the guilt Kevin feels after the accident. How does his guilt compare with the guilt the devil tries to make Alex feel (see page 14)? What does this teach you about guilt and Satan, our accuser?

3. What effect does Dave's conversation with Beth have? How do you think you would have responded to Dave's claim?

4. What does Alex's interaction with Jesus reveal about Jesus? about Alex?

Chapter 3: 72 Hours

1. What do Kevin's stories about Alex's birth and earlier childhood reveal about Alex? about the bond between father and son?

2. Why do you think Pastor Brown's prayer in the waiting room (see page 36) makes such an impact on Kevin?

3. Both Beth and Kevin release Alex to God's care shortly after the accident. Explain when each does so. What effect do you think their prayers of relinquishment have on their sense of peace and hope?

4. Local churches rally around the Malarkeys immediately after the accident. Who is impacted by their service? In what ways?

5. What do you think Alex means when he says, "Heaven is not the next world; it is now" (page 47)?

Chapter 4: An Army Gathers

1. Discuss Kevin's comments on "nice" as applied to Christians and the Christian faith (see page 52). Do you agree that it is "revealing that Jesus, the apostle Paul, and all of the great saints of the Bible were *never* described as nice"? Why or why not?

2. How does 1 John 4:4 ("the Spirit who lives in you is greater than the spirit who lives in the world") apply to the Malarkeys' situation? Have you seen this verse apply to circumstances in your own life? Give examples.

3. What is the tension between science and the sovereignty of God in Alex's story? In what ways (if any) do you feel this tension elsewhere?

4. When Kevin's friend tells Kevin that Alex will become an influential pastor, the friend says, "It makes me as uncomfortable as you seem to be" (see page 62). Why is the friend uncomfortable? Have you ever had to deliver an "uncomfortable" message?

Chapter 5: Miracles, Messes, and More Miracles

1. Discuss Kevin's statement on page 70: "It is one thing to read the Scriptures and affirm their truth. But until you are in the trenches of trial, until you are faced with life circumstances that test your faith, until you are pressed to the absolute limit of your physical and emotional capacity, until you face the unrelenting stress of ongoing trauma, you never really know how you'll respond to what you may have embraced so easily during a comfortable Bible study."

2. Kevin says, "It's ingrained in us to earn our own way, to pay back any little favor, and never to be on the debt side of the ledger" (page 76). If you have ever been "on the debt side of the ledger," how did it feel?

3. Discuss Kevin's father's perspective on Alex's condition. Did it surprise you? Why or why not?

4. Kevin says, "It's possible to know peace and pain at the same time" (page 80) and, "Nothing good ever comes to pass without a price" (page 81). Have you found these statements to be true in your own life? Explain.

5. How does Alex describe angels? Does his description confirm or contradict your own understanding of angels?

Chapter 6: We Meet Another World

1. Discuss the tension Kevin and Beth face as they try to reconcile God's promise that Alex will be healed with the reality of his severe injuries.

2. In what ways do Sue's experience and the artist's painting of angels behind Alex seem to support the Malarkeys belief that God is intervening in time and space to heal Alex?

3. What do you learn about faith from the poem Kevin writes soon after Alex first emerges from his coma (pages 102–103)?

4. Why is the speech therapist's warning that Alex may never be able to respond such a devastating moment for Kevin? How does his analogy to Peter's walking on water apply? Have you ever been in a similar situation? Explain.

5. Discuss Kevin's, Alex's, and Margaret's accounts of the angels in Alex's hospital room.

Chapter 7: Homecomings

1. Does Alex's attitude through his early stages of recovery surprise you? Why or why not?

2. How does Beth respond to Alex's story of the accident? What do you think she took away from that experience?

3. Discuss Kevin's statement with regard to his limited knowledge of what bringing Alex home would entail: "God will be with us whenever we go through deep waters, supplying the grace we

need. Perhaps that's why I didn't know that this was only the first of twelve ambulance trips that Alex and I would take in the next few months" (page 126). Has God ever shown you grace in a similar manner? Explain.

4. How would you sum up the benefits and challenges that come with Alex's going home?

5. What are the results of Kevin and Alex's conversation about the accident? Describe the power of forgiveness in your own life.

6. "[God] was the only reason we had come this far without giving in to utter despair" (page 139). How have you seen this displayed in the Malarkeys' story? How do you maintain hope in difficult situations?

Chapter 8: War and Peace

1. What are your thoughts about the message that Alex "will be fully healed"? Why was Kevin so reluctant to accept it?

2. What might Kevin have missed out on had he not been obedient to the prompting to go forward in church to pray?

3. What does Alex mean when he says, "I'm being attacked"? Have you ever felt attacked by the devil? What does Scripture teach about standing up to Satan's attacks?

4. Why are the Malarkeys uncomfortable with installing a permanent ramp to their house? Is this discomfort justified? Why or why not?

5. What is your reaction to Alex's interacting with angels? to Kevin's reflections on these encounters (see pages 166–169)?

6. How does Alex describe the devil and demons? How does this compare and contrast with how you view them?

Chapter 9: Endings and Beginnings

1. Why is Alex reluctant to share many of his experiences in Heaven? What is your reaction?

2. What is Kevin and Alex's purpose in publishing this book? In your opinion, have they succeeded? Explain.

3. Kevin mentions feeling "supernaturally challenged" (page 185) at times when he interacts with Alex. Have you ever felt that way? Explain.

4. Alex says he knows God is using what happened in the car accident for good. In what ways do you think that is true?

Chapter 10: The Road Ahead

1. What did you learn from the Malarkeys' efforts to include Alex in their everyday activities?

2. What is your response to Kevin's statement, "When God gives you something to do, you just do it. What seems foreign to someone else is normal for us. Every one of us will, to some degree or another, be faced with a new normal sometime in life" (pages 195–196)? Have you ever had to face a "new normal"? Describe that experience and how you dealt with it.

3. Describe Alex's attitude after his surgeries. What is responsible for his outlook?

4. How does Kevin reconcile his belief in Alex's full healing with Alex's not yet being healed today? How might you reconcile these things?